SILICON SHOCK

The Menace of
the Computer Invasion

SILICON SHOCK

The Menace of
the Computer Invasion

Geoff Simons

BASIL BLACKWELL

First published 1985

Basil Blackwell Ltd
108 Cowley Road, Oxford OX4 1JF, UK

Basil Blackwell Inc.
432 Park Avenue South, Suite 1505,
New York, NY 10016, USA

British Library Cataloguing in Publication Data

Simons, Geoff
Silicon stock: the menace of the computer
invasion.
1. Computers and civilization
I. Title
306'.46   QA76.9.C66

Library of Congress Cataloging in Publication Data

Simons, G. L.
Silicon shock.
Bibliography: p.181
Includes index.
1. Computers – Social aspects.
2. Computers –
Psychological aspects.
I. Title.
QA76.9.C66S55   1985   303.4'834   84-29775
ISBN 0-631-13835-8

Typeset by Getset (BTS) Ltd., Eynsham, Oxford
Printed in Great Britain by
The Camelot Press Ltd., Southampton

Contents

Introduction

A woman, in a state of uncontrollable consternation, vomits over a computer terminal.

A man experiences extremes of nausea and giddiness whenever he sees a computer keyboard.

In France, a man rushes into a computer room and shoots the computer.

In the United States, a policeman fires two bullets into a computer terminal.

These events are all true but what do we make of them? Are they isolated and unconnected occurrences, or do they signify a deep underlying apprehension, a suspicion that computers and computer-based systems represent a unique and growing threat to important human values? In the words of an important book – Is the computer *Monster* or *Messiah?*

What we find is a growing apprehension about the role of computers in human society. Many of the anxieties are familiar enough. Will computers put me out of a job? Is addiction to computers affecting social development in children? What if a computer in a military network makes a mistake? Such questions are real enough – indeed they are vital. But there are many other questions to consider, many other ways in which the uncertainties about the computer impact are throwing a shadow over human life. We see that computers are uniquely fitted to serve socially repressive purposes, that they are capable of dehumanizing people in various ways, and – some would say – that they are plotting the extermination of the human race.

It is hardly surprising, in such circumstances, that people

should be fearful of the growing computer encroachment on human activity; and that at times the fear should even result in clinical phobia. The existence of computer phobics is well documented in the literature and we have reason to believe that their ranks are swelling. And it is also significant that phobia is not the only psychiatric condition associated with the proliferation of computers in the modern world. In these pages, in addition to *phobia*, we will also find *depression, allergy, addiction, compulsive neurosis, withdrawal symptoms, illusion, psychological disorientation, delusions of grandeur,* and *megalomania*.

When computers first appeared they were hailed as 'miracle machines', the wonder of the age. Dubbed 'electronic brains', they were widely perceived as having immense mathematical ability, a type of intelligence. The first electronic computers emerged in the 1940s and were based on glass thermionic valves: these tended to be somewhat unreliable but still enabled computers to perform thousands of calculations every second. In the 1950s and 1960s, computers made use of the transistor, first demonstrated in the Bell Laboratories in 1948. By 1970, computers could already store vast amounts of information – and enable it to be retrieved for government, company, military and other purposes. The 1960s saw the arrival of the silicon chip, a wonder of manufacturing technology that allowed hundreds of electronic components to be built on a thin sliver of material: in the early 1970s silicon chips ('integrated circuits') were being manufactured to individually contain about 1000 transistors. And it was the silicon chip that allowed the microprocessor to emerge, the thumbnail-sized 'brain' of the new generation of microcomputers.

Today there is talk of building ten *million*(!) electronic components onto a tiny silicon (or gallium arsenide) chip, of computers that will be able to perform thousands of millions of calculations every second. Already countless files, computerized and often interconnected, are held on private citizens in the developed countries of the world – and many Third World countries are finding that computers are effective in aiding repression. The daunting power of the computer derives not only from its vast memory capacity, but from its developing capacity to manipulate its stored information. Traditional data processing has become effective enough, but today – with the emergence of *artificial intelligence* (AI) and *expert systems* – there is a new disturbing dimension. *Today computers are learning how to think about the information that they hold, how to draw conclusions from their knowledge in ways that are starting to outstrip human intellectual competence.* Already computer experts are beginning to discuss what will happen when computers become capable of intellectual activity that is beyond human comprehension! We should not be surprised that such machines may cause apprehension in human beings. Perhaps we should welcome such anxiety as signalling man's new awareness of a growing threat.

Anxiety about machines is not a new phenomenon. We come to computers with preconceptions, influenced by the humanist and technocratic factors that have helped to shape the culture of the modern world. We find a history of scepticism about the wisdom of consigning more and more functions to mechanical devices – and, in some instances, a veritable war between man and the machine. It has often been perceived that machines can dehumanize people, affecting their self-confidence, their self-image, their freedom in society, and the development of an ethical maturity. The computer bears on all these matters, and more besides.

The computer – *any* modern computer – is skilled at remembering. It can collect *and never forget* facts, numbers, symbols, statements; it can hold statistics and compute trends; it can find connections between items in different files, connections that may have escaped the human operators. It is these sorts of abilities that make the computer so effective at *monitoring and control*. It is this type of talent that makes the computer such a helpful ally for the authoritarian. And the flexibility of computer behaviour enables it to encroach on areas that we may have assumed to be immune from its baleful influence. It can, for example, invade the most intimate areas of human relationships – there are implications here for marriage, personal relations, and sexual fulfilment. Again we can see the computer serving as a dehumanizing force, encouraging people to be machine-focused rather than human-focused.

Underlying all the particular and identifiable threats is the alarming possibility that the computer is evolving beyond human control. Computers are becoming enmeshed in our weaponry, in the systems that advise us when to go to war, and – most dangerous of all – in the very heart of the decision-making machinery that chooses between war and peace. We need only cite the emerging 'launch-on-warning' missile systems, equipped to abolish the bulk of the human race – without a single human being allowed to be involved in the decision-making process. And the prospect of truly intelligent computers being involved in such activity is less than reassuring. Already it is arguable that computers are developing individual autonomy ('free will', as in people), survival instincts, and a prodigious expertise that is already outstripping human competence in many fields. In the sense that we cannot draw theoretical limits around the powers of the supercomputers of tomorrow, then we are seeing the dawn of the *omnipotent machine*.

There is enough here to disturb sensitive folk, though it is likely that such people are already apprehensive. What is described in the present book is a scenario – or a set of scenarios. There are not the only ones possible, though they may appear the ones most likely. It is of course possible that human decision-making may alter the course of machine evolution on this planet, but in the modern world it is hard to imagine a decision of this kind that would not be mediated, at some level, by the involvement of computers themselves. Increasingly we are finding that computers will decide the future of machines on earth – *and also the future of man.*

1

The Coming of Computer Phobia

Preamble

Man is a fear-haunted animal. From the merest frisson of trepidation to the extremes of compulsive phobia there is a spectrum of fear that impinges on all human existence. Through biological evolution we have developed a capacity for fear as a means to survival. We encounter a threat, experience fear, and strive to avoid the hazard. This much is true of countless species, but with *homo sapiens*, perhaps uniquely, there is a further dimension. *In imagination we can conjure dangers.* This affects our emotions and in turn our subsequent actions.

Fear can be typically evoked by different elements in different cultures. Thus we may be constantly anxious about wild animals, the possibility of delayed rains, unemployment or nuclear war. But whatever the specific causes of particular fears and phobias, there is a general anxiety common to all people, a pervasive awareness that the human condition is fragile, insecure, beset by difficulties. This is not a new circumstance. People have always been troubled by thoughts of failure, disease and mortality. The anxiety (*angst, angoisse*) of the existentialist has a perennial relevance. What *is* new is that we are living in the age of modern technology. Today our attitudes are being conditioned by concepts and artefacts of unprecedented power. New machines both aid and threaten our survival as a species: pre-eminent among such devices in the electronic computer.

The computer is immensely versatile: it can be applied with equal facility to any type of well-defined process, such as medical practice, scientific research, traffic control, hotel administration, game playing, circuit design, geological prospecting, war making and countless other tasks. We will see that this versatility has profound implications for human beings in society.

Already it is easy to discern widespread doubts about the wisdom of extending computer power in one domain after another. Already the computer is stimulating new fears and phobias. And we have been aware of this for many years. Some of the anxieties relate to traditional worries about social change and technological innovation. Some, we will see, can be associated with historical suspicions about science, secular philosophy and the ethical status of knowledge itself. Yet others relate to man's self-image as a creative, autonomous being. The computer has the remarkable ability to disturb people, as well as exciting them, on many planes at the same time.

It is a remarkable fact that the computer quickly engages people's emotions. Perhaps they detect a kinship in its developing intellectual abilities. Perhaps, at the same time, they are disturbed by its manifestly alien nature − for whatever a computer can do, however much it may be seen to resemble an intelligent or living creature, it is still essentially removed from the world of human sensitivity and reflection. We will see that people incline either to be alarmed by computers or to be seduced by them into a state of virtual addiction. The computer has the power, not only to engage human emotion, but to push human psychological responses to extremes. In a curious and as yet little explored sense, the computer has 'homed in' on particular vulnerabilities of the human psyche. The computer can generate fear and addiction, phobia and compulsive neurosis.

Computer phobia, as one extreme psychological state among many, it is relatively recent phenomenon in human society − but now it is often described in computer journals and elsewhere. As with other types of phobia it can be characterized by nausea, rapid heart rate, diarrhoea, a desire to urinate, sweating, and a feeling of choking or suffocation. In rare cases there may even be feelings of impending death. A recent issue of the popular computer journal *Computer News* reported an experiment with students at the keyboard of a computer: Sanford Weinburg of St Joseph's University in Pennsylvania found that no less than a third of the students evinced signs of computer phobia.

A phobia is generally represented as a psychological and emotional state characterized by phobic anxiety, where the anxiety involves dread at having to face an object or to be involved in a situation. The dread, usually seen as irrational by a non-phobic observer, leads to strenuous avoidance efforts. Almost any imaginable object can stimulate phobic anxiety: an individual may develop an overpowering fear of other human beings, animals, places, heights, modes of travel, being seen or speaking in public. Consider the following two cases:

> John liked the idea of travel. He wanted to see new places and to meet new people. But he had a problem. He was psychologically unable to cross a bridge, any sort of bridge. To attempt to do so, by walking or using a vehicle, would make his palms sweat, his heart race. On one occasion he had fainted.

> Anne had been a typist for many years. When computer-based word processors were introduced into the office it seemed natural enough to transfer to be new equipment. The new keyboards were identical in layout to those on the old electric typewriters and there were no technical problems. But the first time she tried to use a word processor, she vomited – quite unaccountably and in circumstances of rising panic.

John and Anne are real people (though their names have been changed). Such people are distressed by their condition and can do little to control the rising phobic anxiety in certain well-defined situations. The degree of dread seems out of all proportion to the situation, but the anxiety does not melt away in the light of reason. The only recourse of the sufferer, in the absence of effective therapy, is to avoid the cause of the phobic anxiety. With some types of common phobia (say, snakes or tarantulas) this may be a relatively easy matter for urban dwellers. It is likely to be much more difficult for people with a phobic dread of telephones, cars or computers.

In my acquaintance there are: a shop assistant who shudders at the thought of office automation, a woman who fears that computers will one day 'take over', a commercial manager who hates computers because they baffle him. Such people are symptomatic of a growing trend, a new anxiety directed at increasingly competent machines. Often it seems difficult to communicate the nature of the trepidation, the precise flavour of the persistent unease. But the phobic symptoms, albeit in an early stage of development, are unmistakable: sudden emotional reaction when computers are mentioned, avoidance behaviour in conversation or physical movement, persistent and deepening attitudes despite evidence that may pull in an opposite direction. Terms such as *'robotphobia'*, *'cyberphobia'* and *'computerphobia'* have started to appear in the general and technical literature. Technological innovation, perhaps for peculiar reasons, is adding to the spectrum of items and situations that can generate phobic anxiety in susceptible people.

Many phobic sufferers are ashamed of their condition. They recognize the seeming irrationality behind the distressing symptoms and they may even be driven to doubt their sanity. The phobic anxiety, unlike common fears, may make it virtually impossible to conduct a normal life: the agoraphobic may become a virtual recluse, sometimes not only fearful of open spaces but also of the chance encounter with other people; and the person who experiences rising panic at the thought of machines or electricity is forced to live with constant apprehension and feelings of helplessness.

Common fears lubricate the business of life, motivating the individual to avoid hazard; phobias cause social paralysis and desperate avoidance, rendering life permanently troubled and unmanageable. Fears are frequent but do not interfere with life; phobias are less frequent but impair the life of the sufferer and so also the lives of relatives and friends. Men and women tend to share common fears, but female phobics are more numerous than male. Children are less likely to suffer from phobic anxiety than are adults. Not surprisingly, phobias that focus on machines in general and computers in particular are more common in urban developed countries than in areas that are rural and poor. It is useful to glance at the spectrum of phobia in history and today to understand better its relevance to the modern technological age.

The Spectrum of Phobia

Fear is much older than *homo sapiens*: prehuman species developed a capacity for fear to help them survive. But can non-human animals experience phobia? We will not ask the animal-lovers since to them *animal* can almost be equated with *human* (except where humans choose to act in a 'bestial' fashion). A woman on radio claimed that her dog suffered from agoraphobia, but perhaps this canine condition was caused by the rigours of urban society. It is difficult to speculate on how we would recognize evidence for animal phobia in prehuman or contemporary species.

The earliest account of human phobia can be found in the writings of Hippocrates, the so-called father of modern medicine, who lived four centuries before Christ. Hippocrates described a man (an evident *acrophobic*) who 'could not go near a precipice or over a bridge, or beside even the shallowest ditch'. And he also noted a man who was phobic of flutes, but only at night. As soon as the first note was heard, the man would be terrified; but if the instrument were played in the daylight hours then the man would be completely untroubled. In another section, Hippocrates describes someone who 'through bashfulness, suspicion and timorousness, will not be seen abroad; loves darkness as life and cannot endure the light or to sit in lightsome places; his hat still in his eyes, he will neither see, nor be seen by his good will.' The social phobia of this man is unmistakable: 'He dare not come in company for fear he should be misused, disgraced, overshoot himself in gesture or speeches, or be sick; he thinks every man observes him . . ..'

In his famous *Anatomy of Melancholy*, published in 1621, Robert Burton wrote of the phobic reaction: 'Many lamentable effects this causeth in men, as to be red, pale, tremble, sweat . . .. They that live in fear are never free, resolute, secure, never marry, but in continual pain . . . no greater misery, no rack, no torture, like unto it.' He described the differences between depression and fear, and mentioned historical figures who may be regarded as having suffered from phobic reactions, such as Tully and Demosthenes (both of whom commonly experienced stagefright) and Augustus Caesar (who could not bear to sit in the dark). Burton described a patient who would

> not walk alone from home, for fear he should swoon, or die. A second fears every man he meets will rob him, quarrel with him, or kill him. A third dare not venture to walk alone, for fear he should meet the devil, a thief, be sick . . . another dares not go over a bridge, come near a pool, brook, steep hill, lye in a chamber where cross-beams are, for fear he be tempted to hang, drown or precipitate himself.

The same man was worried that he may say something indecent during a sermon, or be sick or faint for no good cause (for this reason he still carried 'bisket, aquavitae, or some strong waters about him'). And he was terrified that he would be trapped in the middle of a church or a crowd of people ('he is so mis-affected').

It became common to describe phobias in historical writings and other literature. King James I of England was said to be terrified at the sight of an unsheathed sword, causing a witness to remark that 'Elizabeth was King, James I was Queen'. Another king, Germanicus, experienced phobic anxiety at the sight or sound of cocks. And when syphilis ravaged Europe, phobic reactions were common. Thus in 1721 a physician described syphilophobia: 'If but a pimple appears or any slight ache is felt, they distract themselves with terrible apprehensions: by which means they make life uneasy to themselves and run for help . . ..' And the violent and persistent character of the phobia is evident: 'And so strongly are they for the most part possessed with this notion that an honest practitioner generally finds it more difficult to cure the imaginary evil than the real one.'

Henry III of France and the Duke of Schonberg feared cats, and the Empress Catherine of Russia was obliged to give an audience to a famous general in a room bereft of mirrors. The Italian writer Manzoni, an evident agoraphobic, feared that he would faint whenever he left his house, and so carried a bottle of concentrated vinegar at all times. The French playwright Feydeau feared daylight, and Sigmund Freud experienced phobic anxiety in connection with travel. Phobia, like fear, runs indelibly through the history of human society.

Today there is an abundant literature on phobias and related conditions (for example, look at any volume of *Psychological Abstracts*). Most of the material deals with new therapeutic efforts, though the objects and situations that generate phobic anxiety are much the same as those reported in the historical literature. People can still be terrified of animals, closed spaces, heights, public places and other individuals. They can still panic when required to cross a bridge, enter a wood, or address a group of people.

There is no limit to the range of objects and situations that can generate a phobic response in susceptible people. Most of us are acquainted with fear of snakes (ophidiophobia) and fear of spiders (arachneophobia), but we may be surprised to learn that terror may be induced by drinking (dypsophobia), fish (ichthyophobia) and rain (ombrophobia). It is even possible to be phobic about the possibility of being phobic, a condition termed *phonophobic*; or to suffer from a fear of everything (panophobia).

Hundreds of different phobias are now recognized by clinical practitioners, and books on the subject typically list a few dozen types with their medical names. It is possible to be phobic about flowers, glass or heat; cats, pregnancy or women; nakedness, rivers or solitude. It is even possible to suffer from ergophobia, extreme anxiety at the thought of work – though employers may be reluctant to take this one seriously. Being touched, being wet, sitting down, seeing colours, thinking about teeth, feeling the wind – all can generate phobic anxiety in some people. We cannot imagine an item, a situation or an experience that is not the cause of phobia in some sufferer. And we have already seen that there are some 'blanket' phobias – phobophobia and panophobia – that can impinge on the whole of human existence.

Some of the modern phobias are new, focusing as they do on technological innovation. It is not uncommon today to find people who experience panic when expected to use a lift, a train or an aeroplane. We can see why such things should cause fear in some people but there is still none the less an irrational element in the phobic response. A wide range of other technological entities can also cause fear: it is not unknown for individuals to dread the telephone, the television receiver in the corner of the room, or the electric bell on the front door. And we have already instanced the growing prevalence of computer phobia.

There are a number of specific anxieties that are relevant to the possibility of phobia in this area. One need only think of neophobia (fear of anything new), electrophobia (fear of electricity) and mechanophobia (fear of machines). Where a computer is personalized – i.e. viewed in anthropomorphic terms – it may generate a phobic response that is normally caused by contact with another human being. Similarly, if (like Joseph Weizenbaum, 1976) we are able to view a computer as an *organism*, then the machine may generate the sort of phobia that is normally evoked by animals. Or, conversely, if the computer encourages a person to neglect social contact, a condition of autophobia (fear of being alone) may develop in due course; if, alternatively, the computer proves to be a quite sufficient companion, then the seeds of anthrophobia (fear of other human being) may develop in the obsessive programmer, the *hacker*. Treated in this speculative fashion, the computer is clearly a potentially fertile source of phobic conditions. At the same time the computer is helping us to understand human psychology.

Computers and Psychology

The 1940s saw the arrival of electronic digital computers, a development that was to profoundly affect views about human psychology. It was already evident that the new electronic devices could do many of the things that were formerly the prerogative of human beings and other intelligent animals. For example, computers could learn, store and manipulate information, solve problems, take decisions, and carry out a range of simple reasoning tasks. In the 1950s a number of influential publications encouraged the development of a computer model for human psychology. Miller (1956) published a seminal paper which explored the information-processing characteristics of the human mind; and Newell *et al.* (1958) and other researchers were beginning to reframe the traditional psychological questions in terms of metaphors derived from the rapidly evolving computer science. One significant innovation, associated with Miller and co-workers, was that the unit of behaviour could be regarded as a *plan*, a behaviour-generating system similar to the typical feedback loops used in computers. Here man is depicted as an active processor of information, not simply a passive recipient of incoming data. In 1971 Earl Hunt asked 'What kind of a computer is man?' and attempted to describe a computing system that 'thinks like a man'. It was obvious that computers were telling us more about the human mind, and the new computer-inspired models were enlarging our ideas about what computers themselves could become. Allport in 1980 declared that the advent of artificial intelligence, a subclass of computer science, 'is the single most important development in the history of psychology'.

What we see is a conflux of influences – deriving from computer science, information theory, new linguistic ideas (Chomsky), new notions about cognitive development (Piaget), etc. – stimulating the emergence of information-processing psychology. This new approach, quickly dubbed *cognitivism* or *cognitive psychology*, is today the most influential school of psychology. Does it have anything to say about mental disturbance in general and phobia in particular?

In the cognitive model of the human mind, information is received by the system, held in buffer stores or permanent memory, processed according to intelligent routines, and used to initiate behavioural and other responses. Fear and other emotions may be depicted as cognitive states that influence the processing of certain types of information (we cannot pursue here the cognitive theory of emotion, but see Strongman, 1979, pp. 34 – 49). A phobia may be represented as a disproportionate weighting of certain processing factors in the system. Phobia is only 'fear writ large' and this very metaphor suggests that quantitative factors, laid up in the neural pathways, are likely to be responsible for the disproportionate emotional response to certain common (and less common) objects and experiences. This is no explanation of phobia but it suggests a framework that could yield new metaphors and fresh research programmes.

It would, for example, be a relatively straightforward matter to model human phobia in computer systems. Boden (1977) discusses the simulation of neurosis in computer programs, and other forms of mental disability are clearly amenable to the same sort of treatment. It would be intriguing if an explanation of *computer phobia* were to emerge through a simulation of phobia in computer programs. And this scenario is not entirely fanciful. One of the great strengths of modern cognitive psychology is that it becomes possible to investigate internal mental structures – in terms of how computer programs, written to perform in 'mental' ways, are put together. It is highly likely that the computer model of the human mind will illuminate not only the normal psychological workings but also those types of operations and responses that are usually deemed worthy of psychiatric investigation.

However, before we accomplish a full explanation of (computer) phobia, and other mental conditions via the computer software route, we can identify a number of considerations that will be relevant to this sort of enquiry. What has already emerged is that phobias are peculiar phenomena: they take on an individual character according to the character of the sufferer, the particular circumstances, and the nature of the feared object. We would expect an explanation of ereuthophobia (fear of blushing) in a teenage girl to differ in important respects from an explanation of taphephobia (fear of being buried alive) in a ninety-year-old recluse. Similarly, we would expect an explanation of computer phobia to have characteristic features, though these would vary according to the circumstances and character of the sufferer and according also to the precise nature of the phobia itself: the diminutive lurking micro, hidden away in this or that piece of domestic equipment, may be expected to sire a different sort of anxiety to that occasioned by a mighty Cray computer, capable of a thousand million operations a second.

If we are looking for common elements in computer phobia there are various candidates, and it is perhaps significant that these can also be found in the literature dealing with other types of phobia. We have already mentioned some of these factors but it is worth considering them in more detail. There are at least three types of factors that appear relevant to most, if not all, species of computer phobia.

Fear of the new (neophobia, kainophobia, kainotophobia)

Computers are nothing if not new. All the computer generations – and now we are developing the fifth – have been packed into about forty years. New computer systems and new applications are today bursting upon us at a prodigious rate.

The need to retain personal control

People need to feel that they are, to a significant extent, in control of their own lives. Anything that militates against this urge – slavery, dictatorship, arbitrary management decisions, etc. – is rightly perceived as a threat. Computers are now encroaching on one area of personal control after another. This, perceived by human beings, is resented and feared.

Fear of machines (mechanophobia)

This, as we have seen, may be linked in the modern age to fear of electricity (electrophobia). We will say nothing more about mechanophobia at this stage. There are many reasons why people have learnt to fear machines in general (chapter 2) and why they are learning to fear computers in particular (chapters 3 to 6).

These three factors are not the only ones that can be imagined, but they appear central to computer phobia. We need to give them some attention.

Fearing the New

We have long known the new and the strange to be sources of anxiety. The human infant is quickly startled and ready to cry at any sudden or novel stimulus, and it is generally reckoned that between the ages of 6 and 12 months most normal infants begin to develop a fear of strangers. In fact the fear of the strange is a cross-species phenomenon. The Canadian researcher Hebb showed how chimpanzees were terrified by a plaster death mask taken from one of their number who had recently died. Strange masks and other unfamiliar objects are likely to frighten young children in certain circumstances. And sometimes novel stimuli can attract and repel in turn, a possibility described by Konrad Lorenz in connection with the raven: 'A young raven, confronted with a new object, which may be a camera, an old bottle, a stuffed polecat, or anything else, first reacts with escape responses.' Later, if the object does not prove to be hostile, the bird will explore it with growing confidence; finally, 'He will grab it with one foot, peck at it, try to tear off pieces . . .', and then carry it off to some convenient hole.

Various researchers have proposed that strangeness is one of the main determinants of fear. Thus many animals accept new objects and new territory to the extent that they are familiar with them. If an animal has spent a lengthy time in one environment, a new environment will be all the stranger. Novel or unexpected stimuli are disturbing to many species. And it has been pointed out that any perception of 'strangeness' must presuppose that a framework of the 'familiar and what is to be expected' has already been established. Thus in very young chicks and very young babies the scope for anxiety is much less than in their older siblings. In human adults there is often anxiety caused by unfamiliar items or events which upset the comfortable routine of life or which cannot be explained. There is much evidence of this in the anthropological literature.

The Dakotas, one of the old Indian tribes in North America, used to refer to their deities by the term *waken*, which was also used for anything that could not be understood or was marvellous and superhuman. It is interesting also that the Maori word for god is *atua*, a term also used for whatever is incomprehensible (such as the compass and the barometer, and even menstruation). In the South Celebes, the word *pemali* denotes any item or event which is regarded as a subject for taboo; significantly, it also signifies anything unusual which is likely to bring evil consequences. Crawley (1902), from whom these examples are culled, emphasizes how strangeness and potential danger can go together 'in the savage mind'.

The American Indians and other primitive groups have tended to regard any remarkable features of natural scenery as necessarily dangerous. Sir Everard Im Thurn has said of the Guiana Indian that if 'he sees anything in any way curious or abnormal, and if soon after an evil befall him, he regards the thing and the evil as cause and effect . . ..' In a similar spirit, the Ainu of Japan used to deify all objects which appeared unusual or dreadful, to neutralize thereby any baleful consequences. Westermarck (1912–1917) pointed out:

> the superstitious dread of unusual objects is not altogether dead even among ourselves. It survives in England to this day in the habit of ascribing grotesque and striking landmarks or puzzling antiquities to the devil, who became the residuary legatee of obsolete superstitions in Christian countries.

And where unusual objects could generate fear and an expectation of evil consequences, so uncommon or strange individuals could evoke dread. We have seen how infants may fear strangers, but such anxieties are far from absent in adults. Dobrizhoffer (in the *Historia de Abiponibus*, 1784) recorded how the primitive Guaranis associated every stranger with hostility; and Laval (in the *Annales de la Propagation de la Foi*, 1837) wrote how newly arrived missionaries in the Gambier lands were regarded by the natives as malevolent gods come to do harm, just as the Polynesians regarded all foreigners as bringers of disease. The Samoans were said to fear the evil influence of strangers, and the Maoris needed to carry out purification ceremonies to neutralize the dangers inherent in any new territory. Sir Richard Burton cited linguistic evidence to demonstrate the widespread dislike of strangers. Hence the Hebrew Goyi (Gentile), the Hindu Mlenchla (mixed or impure breed), and the Chinese Fan Kwei (foreign devil). Anyone who doubts that such zenophobic attitudes are present in the world today should reflect on how the French and the Argentinians have been popularly regarded by the British people in recent years.

There is also a cross-cultural recognition of the hazards of carrying out an act for the first time. Thus we may experience anxiety when first learning to drive a car, swimming an unusually long distance, or first addressing a large group of people. People coming to a computer keyboard for the first time have reported fears that the machine *'might do something unexpected'* or that *'they might break it'*. Something being done for the first time is universally seen as fraught with hazard. There is continuity in this between the past and the present, between savage communities and modern man.

The Guiana Indians felt compelled to arrest the ill-will of the spirits before attempting to shoot a cataract for the first time; sometimes, when entering a new place, the Indians would blind their eyes with pepper juice to avoid the dangers of casting eyes on a new environment. The Sandwich Islanders worried about starting to till the ground, about casting the first nets, about launching the first boats; the natives of the Luang Sermata Islands worried about new houses – would they bring bad luck? And similar anxieties were described by Pinkerton in his writings about nineteenth-century journeys through Persia and China.

The new and the strange – whether in the form of environmental features, human strangers, peculiar objects, or freshly contrived artefacts – have always had the capacity to arouse anxiety in people. There is much in this that is relevant to the human response to technological innovation in modern society. Computers in particular are new and strange, and possessed of remarkable potential for impinging on human lives. And computers are possessed also of mysterious powers that baffle not only the computer-naive observer but also, we will see, the computer initiate. It is obvious why computers can cause anxiety in many different areas of the human psyche: it homes in, with uncanny precision, on many of the sources of anxiety that have troubled people in different cultures and different ages. The computer can easily be cast as a malevolent and mysterious force, having profound environmental and human consequences but little understood and difficult to placate. When we confidently proclaim that the computer is 'only a machine', we suspect that it is none the less different in some profoundly important ways to a typewriter or a motor vehicle. In being new and strange, the computer feeds that *amorphous anxiety* that human beings have always known; and we will see that there are *particular* computer-generated anxieties that are easy to describe.

The Need for Control

People naturally resent what they perceive to be a diminution of control over their own lives, their own destiny. They like to be able to choose their own clothes, their own occupations, their own friends. In reality the area of choice is heavily constrained, but there is still a ubiquitous human appetite for personal autonomy, for a situation in which people do not feel 'ordered about', subject to arbitrary police or employer decisions, subject to any manner of social or personal repression. It is a common-place of management theory, if not practice, that workers should be involved in decision-making, allowed a voice in the control of corporate development. There is a consensus that people feed a need to control the various factors that affect their lives. And even where a structured framework is desirable or comforting, the computer has an insidious impact on human life. It reduces people to cogs in the social machine.

Many phobias – for example, traumatophobia (fear of injury) and thanatophobia (fear of death) – can be directly linked to anxieties about loss of control. If people are disabled or dead their capacity to exercise control over anything is at least severely reduced. And it is easy to see that computers are evolving to reduce the areas of human control in many social sectors. There is an increasing tendency – in social administration, government decision-making, financial planning, war-making, etc. – to allow computers a judgemental role; and, in such areas as police surveillance and employment, computers are either impinging on civil liberties or effectively performing a wide range of tasks that were once the sole province of human workers (see chapter 3). In such ways computers are gradually encroaching on the areas of personal control.

Such a development is highly relevant to many aspects of the human outlook. It influences attitudes to goals, the concept of purpose, and the framing of an acceptable self-image. Laura Perls (1970), in common with other writers, has pointed out that man is suspended between two poles; awareness that each individual is a unique person, and awareness that every person will die. The first of these brings an element of comfort, the second little but fear and frustration. But if the individual's uniqueness, the precious personal sense of identity, is once removed then there is nothing to counter the inevitable terrors of mortality. It may well be that the computer, by progressively rendering obsolescent one human skill after another, has the power to prevent human beings from exercising control over any aspect of their lives. People gain satisfaction ('self-actualization') through the purposeful development of skills and talents. This is a circumstance that computers could affect in profoundly adverse ways.

The Fear of Machines

Mechanophobia (fear of machines) can take many forms: there is an immense spectrum of machines, and their effects on human society are numerous and multi-dimensional. Particular machines may be feared for particular reasons. Aircraft, for example, may be feared because of a horror of flying; or a television may evoke anxiety because it is known to consume electricity. An explanation of one type of mechanophobia may be totally inadequate for another: we may suspect that an analysis of computer phobia will have little to say about amaxophobia (a fear of vehicles). Since machines were first contrived, man has viewed them with ambivalence. The emergence of the computer has served to heighten the uncertainty and the anxiety.

The Emergence of Computers

It was during the Second World War that electronic computers first impinged on human endeavour. What were called 'automatic computers' were built at Bletchley to carry out cryptoanalysis (code-breaking) tasks for the British Foreign Office, and the huge ENIAC machine – comprising 18,000 unreliable vacuum tubes, weighing more than 30 tons, and having less power than a modern home computer – was commissioned in 1945 for the US Army Ordnance Department to perform ballistics calculations. Perhaps we should not be too surprised that the first computers were employed for military purposes.

During the 1950s and 1960s, computers were increasingly adopted by banks and insurance companies to carry out straightforward financial calculations, and it was during this period that the first doubts about computers were expressed. Much of the concern focused on the employment question (Would the new technology push ever greater numbers of people into redundancy?), but other anxieties were also voiced. It became fashionable to dub the new machines 'electronic brains' and they quickly acquired a totally misplaced reputation for infallibility and omnipotence. In fanciful speculation, computers would one day 'take over', come to rule man, be totally indifferent to human feelings. At the time there were few grounds for such thoughts, but today we can see that the early anxieties showed remarkable prescience. There is more than one sense in which computers are evolving to become the dominant intelligence on this planet (see, for example, discussion of the 'artificial expert' in chapter 6). This circumstance has far-reaching implications for human society.

The early enthusiasm for computers – usually either a commercial or military commitment – was soon tempered in various ways as the doubts began to emerge. Were computers really more efficient, in all their applications, than the former manual methods? Would there be adverse consequences for employment, job satisfaction, social relations? Were there hidden dangers in assigning an ever larger range of tasks to intelligent machines? Over the last three decades such questions have been asked with growing frequency, and in the more obvious areas of concern (e.g. the impact of technology on employment) there is already a prodigious literature. And there are ways in which the questions are becoming more important. As computers develop, they are acquiring a dramatically enlarged spectrum of competence: it is now increasingly realistic to expect computers to adopt roles that require *real* intelligence or a capacity for judgemental decision-making. We have scarcely begun to address ourselves to the implications of this type of development.

Many of the recent empirical studies on the social impact of computers show both adverse and beneficial consequences. For example, Kling (1982) in a detailed literature survey shows a massive range of influences, many of which accord with doubts expressed in the early days of computing. Some of the worries focus on the technical failures of systems. For example, with computerized banking what would be the consequences of a 'credit blackout' caused by electrical failure? And it is easy to speculate in a similar vein about the effects of technical failure in an air-traffic control network, in a computerized intensive-care unit, or in a 'launch-on-warning' military defence complex. And where computer-based systems are technically robust and reliable there can still be many grounds for concern.

Some researchers have investigated aspects of work life unrelated to the broad questions of employment and redundancy. Braverman (1974), for instance, suggests that managers see workers as general-purpose machines which they operate: where computers are introduced into an organization, they represent another type of machine which can enhance management power and weaken the power of lower-level participants in the organization. And clearly, in this framework it is very much in management interest to replace unreliable and recalcitrant human beings (inefficient 'machines') with superior computer-based machines that are unlikely to become bored or to join trade unions. Such an attitude was well represented in the culture before the time when electronic computers were a practical possibility. Hence in *Erewhon*, first published in 1872, Samuel Butler observes:

> the machine is brisk and active, when the man is weary; it is clear-headed and collected, when the man is stupid and dull; it needs no slumber, when man must sleep or drop; ever at its post, ever ready for work, its alacrity never flags, its patience never gives in

And Rotwang, the evil scientist/magician in the classic film *Metropolis* (1926), proclaims with delight: 'I have created a machine in the image of man, that never tires or makes a mistake . . . Now we have no further use for living workers.' There are many ways in which computers extend the control of one group over another, serving to entrench existing hierarchies and to exacerbate tensions between one job or grade in an organization and another.

Computers may also generate problems that may not have been anticipated. A computer-based system may work perfectly but at the same time not be well suited to the intended application. (Again there is a massive literature on designing 'tailor-made' computer systems.) It may be difficult or impossible to design a suitable computer system for a particular purpose. Some of the operating factors may be 'ill-defined', 'informal' or 'fuzzy'. Alter (1980) discovered an array of recurrent problems in computer-based systems which he variously attributed to the technology, the quality of the data used, inadequate system conceptions and people. This is an interesting observation: we may take it as quaint or alarming, according to viewpoint, that *'people'* can be depicted as a problem in computer-based systems.

There is also the question of *incomprehensible programs*. One of the most remarkable features of the most complex modern computer systems is that *nobody understands them*. We will not explore this circumstance here (see chapter 5), except to indicate some of the questions that it raises. If systems are not fully understood, even by computer specialists, are we right to rely on them? How are users to interact with software that they cannot begin to comprehend? How can we begin to ensure that incomprehensible computer programs serve human interest rather than storing up immense hazard for the future? There are vital questions here that are too rarely addressed.

Nor are the anxieties of computer users allayed by their typical contact with the computer world. It has been emphasized (for example, by Kling, 1982) that many of the difficulties that users face in exploiting computer-based systems lie in how the computing package – the complex of hardware, software, skills, organizational units, prevailing beliefs about computing, etc. – is 'embedded in a complex web of social relationships'. This means that misunderstandings can arise, intended objectives are not achieved, and people lose confidence in what was intended to be a problem-solving strategy.

Complex data bases bring their own difficulties. Thus swollen data bases may be seen as a troublesome phenomenon, and there is much evidence that automated information systems often supply inadequate data to their users (see, for example, Danziger, 1977; Dery, 1977). Sometimes supplied data is inappropriate or irrelevant to an enquiry, or the data cannot be cross-referenced in useful ways. In the worse cases, data may be totally out-of-date or factually wrong (there are the sorts of concerns that have stimulated privacy legislation in many developed countries). And where data bases are *not* over loaded or badly designed, there are fresh causes for concern. What do the data bases contain? Is there a body of personal data which should not be on file? Who can access the data base? Are the routes of access technically appreciated by those people charged with the tasks of introducing protective legislation? How can we know what is going on?

The inefficiencies and dangers of computerized information systems can reinforce the threats to civil liberties (see chapter 3). Kraemer *et al.* (1980) found that, using computerized information facilities, police were more likely to detain people who should not have been detained and to arrest people who should not have been arrested. There is an evident price to be paid for using computers to achieve 'more efficient' police activities.

Already we see a disturbing catalogue of doubts about the efficacy of computer use in human society. There are circumstances in which computers can variously threaten employment, job satisfaction, health, civil liberties and the very survival of society. From the relatively trivial billing errors (Sterling, 1979) to the incomprehensible programs of Weizenbaum (1976) there is a spectrum of computer obtuseness that is an ample source of human fear and phobia. It is hardly surprising that we are constantly asked: 'Can we adjust to computer culture?' (*New Scientist*, 14 April 1983). Here we find a description of a New York Academy of Science conference on 'Computer Culture': in the Empire State Ballroom a host of computer-naïve people were addressed by such computer experts as Marvin Minsky and Edward Feigenbaum. The *New Scientist* reporters commented: 'By Friday, after four days of being enthused at, confused, intrigued and occasionally feeling rather excited, the 800 delegates must have been glad to think of one computerized future that was just different *rather than scary*' (my italics). Contact with the computer visionaries did little, it seems, to allay the natural anxieties about the course of computer evolution.

Alongside the many undeniable advantages of computerization it appears that computers represent a multifaced threat to human equanimity. Because of their versatile application potential there is virtually no area which can remain immune to computer encroachment, and this circumstance inevitably affects how human purpose is framed in society. Why bother to play chess when a computer can beat you? Why bother to learn maths when a mathematical *expert system* will always prove faster and more competent? Why bother to learn the violin when a computer-based music synthesizer will replicate not only the sound of the violin but the sound of any instrument we know and some we cannot imagine? Computers represent a broad-based threat to human self-esteem, and their evolution has scarcely begun. It would be remarkable, in the circumstances of a multifaceted computer threat to human status, social life and survival, if we could not detect signs of computer fear and phobia. In fact there are already many such signs and these will increase in number as computer evolution gathers pace.

Computer Phobia

General

Evidence for computer phobia sometimes appears in unexpected places. Thus in an issue of *Sounds* (18 February 1984), the popular-music magazine, we find the following declaration about computers: 'Like sharks 10 years ago, computers have taken over the world. Also like sharks, most people are TERRIFIED of them.' And sometimes the terror, or anger, leads to action. In August 1978 an unhappy postal inspector rushed into the computer room of Montpellier's main post office, in Southern France, and opened fire on the computer. It was damaged by five bullets – the reports did not say whether it suffered fatal injuries – while the sole human employee present had the wisdom to hide under a table. Elsewhere in Europe and in America, computers have been attacked as symbols of repressive authority.

There are also many fictional stories in which vulnerable human beings struggle to cope with fearful computers, robots and other malevolent machines (see chapter 3). A central thread in a recent stage play – *Alice* by Richard Scott (with music by Anthony Phillips), shown in March 1984 at the Leeds Playhouse – focused unambiguously on computer phobia. Here Alice, an ordinary Level 8 programmed microchip, is exhorted to escape from the computer program in the hands of the Queen. In due course, with the help of the Mathmagician, she manages to free herself, whereupon her life assumes what we take to be more human facets – in this case: wine, men and song.

The *Alice* message is clear enough. Computers represent arbitrary power over human lives; the robot is akin to Orwell's 'thought police'; and to be programmed is to be constrained, partial and inhuman. The only solution is to escape from the restrictive computer influence into spontaneous human activity. The contrast between a programmed robot-like response and truly worthwhile creative endeavour is one that is often encountered in philosophy and art.

The difficulty in coping with intelligent machines is graphically highlighted by the *'Who's in charge?'* question. Where a human being uses a complex computer system, who is really controlling the transaction – the person or the intelligent machine? Most people will find this an easy question to answer: surely, since the computer has no autonomy, it is the human being that controls the situation. But we will see that this is a simplistic view. Human unease at the power of the computer is often evident, and there is even a sense in which we can detect an emerging computer autonomy, a capacity in automatic systems for taking 'free' decisions (see chapter 7). In the early days of computers it was fashionable to dub them 'electronic brains' and to imagine that they had minds of their own. Today, when such a claim can be made with more justification, computers can be intimidating creatures.

A businesswoman working with computers has been quoted (in Heller and Bower, 1983): 'It's scary to feel that you aren't in control, that you have absolutely no understanding of what the machine is going to do, and if it will ever do what you want it to!' And the fear that computers will replace human beings in one job after another is often cited. Here we can often discern truly phobic reactions. For example, one woman who supervised accounting clerks was asked by her management to use a computer. She observed: 'I thought the computers were going to replace us and that I would be the first to go. Until we clarified the situation, *I got physically sick every time I went near the computer!*' (my italics).

The fear of being replaced by a computer is often accompanied by a range of other related anxieties. A report from the US consultancy firm International Resource Development (mentioned in *Computer Talk*, 11 April 1983) has indicated the fears that many workers have about computers. In addition to the possibility of being replaced by a machine, there are various other aspects that cause concern. People who are anxious about their literacy and numeracy abilities may worry about having to work with computers: there is a peculiar 'computer mystique' that can be very discouraging to employees and other individuals who have little confidence in their levels of academic attainment. People may fear failure when using a computer (*'Will the computer go berserk?'*, *'Will it blow up if I press the wrong button?'*). And the worker may feel that he has less control over his work than previously, and fewer ways to check his own performance. The psychologist David Ledecky, responsible for various computer-oriented reports in the USA, has commented: 'A great deal of this compuphobia can be related to math anxiety and to difficulties that individuals encounter in learning foreign languages.' For example, the need for programmers to learn even a simple computer language, such as BASIC, shows that the truly 'user-friendly' computer is not yet with us.

Many people trying to learn about computers are intimidated by the task, and some of them may be *cyberphobes*. Thus Anderson (1983), after beginning his article with the provocative 'What – me a cyberphobe?', points out that people in the beginner category are making an effort to educate themselves, 'but are intimidated, whether or not they openly admit it'. And he emphasizes that intimidation, 'with its longtime partner, fear, are extremely effective blockers of learning'. Moreover, the claims of the computer enthusiasts – *compuphiles* – can also be disturbing. Isaac Asimov, for example, has argued that when a computer is built up of an equal number of equally complex cells to those in the human brain, 'in an equally complex arrangement, we will have something that can do *just as much as a human brain can do to its uttermost genius*' (my italics). This idea can be disturbing to many people (Anderson: 'Those are the kinds of assertions that evoke, unknowingly and unintentionally, grave consternation among the cyberphobic'). It is bad enough that we may have difficulty in understanding how computers work. How are we to react to predictions that they will become as competent as human beings?

In short, computers can be perceived as threatening in many ways. They represent a powerful presence in society and often seem to be wresting control from man himself. They seem to be encroaching on our lives, inexorably and unceasingly, finding their way not only into our domestic equipment but also into our bodies (witness the microprocessor-controlled heart pacemakers). The ubiquitous character of the computer can be a threatening element, particularly when we can perceive no theoretical constraint on the versatility of its application. Sometimes human beings seem remarkably vulnerable when they are forced to interact with computer-based systems: people may be forced to trust *blindly*, and in circumstances of diminishing self-confidence, in the deliverances of the automated facility. And sometimes human vulnerability can result in death. A leading Japanese newspaper, the *Ashai Shimbun* (mentioned in *Computing*, 8 July 1982), has reported that there have now been several accidents with robots, 'resulting in death' and 'many more cases just short of accidents'.

Working with computer-based systems can also result in uncommon levels of stress, a circumstance that would expect to feed computer phobia. The term 'computer crazies' has been coined to denote those so afflicted. A Los Angeles psychologist, Thomas McDonald, reckons to have traced a number of anxieties and marital troubles back to the computer. He has suggested that people become psychologically disoriented when working with computers, and attitudes to human relationships can become distorted. What is clear is that computers have a considerable psychological impact on the human scene: they are not neutral in such matters, but can create new attitudes, influence established modes of thought, and have a moral impact on human lives, even though we must assume that at present computers are totally *a*moral systems.

Where a ubiquitous and powerful element in society can have such far-reaching consequences, we would expect it to generate emotional responses in human beings. Some feelings are positive, sympathetic and enthusiastic about technological innovation; other computer-stimulated feelings are negative, anxious and fearful. But there may be a peculiar unity in these disparate reactions. (Certain types of people are expected to be at once 'God-fearing' and capable to an enduring 'love of God'. The God-fearing citizen is quite likely to proclaim that 'God is Love', a seeming paradox that may signal a deeper psychological truth.) Perhaps the obsessive hacker and the computer-phobe are, if not twin-brothers, at least cousins. It is obvious that the computer is a highly potent psychological factor, able to stimulate both obsessional commitment and phobic hostility in the same human society.

A Word about Terminology

There is a growing recognition of the incidence of computer phobia, though people often mean different things when they use the phrase. Anderson (1983) comments that *'cyberphobia'* is now a term 'of growing usage, import and incidence'. And by this word he understands 'chronic anxiety' about computers. Chin (1983), after mentioning *'cyberphobia'* ('the fear of computers'), also introduces us to *'technophobia'*, *'computerphobia'* and *'cryptophobia'*. We are assured that such terms should not simply refer to *'computer cowardice'* but to a complex phobia in its truest sense, involving strong emotional and physical responses. For example, a striving for avoidance is a characteristic phobic response: 'In the case of cyberphobia, it's eluding a cold piece of hardware at all costs.' Mike Legut, a San Francisco therapist cited by Chin, reckons that the vast increase in computer-related jobs will result in a growing number of cyberphobic cases.

Heller and Bower (1983) regard *computerphobia* as 'negative feelings, stereotypes, or preconceptions about computers . . .', a general categorization that would allow many people to qualify. Indeed, Professor Sanford Weinberg of St Joseph's University in Philadelphia has estimated that as many as 30 per cent of the US population are *cyberphobiacs* ('people who fear computers'). One response to the Weinberg figure suggests that it may be a much exaggerated estimate. Thus Stone and Barker (1983) declare: 'I flatly reject this projection. Based on my experience, I offer 3% as a more appropriate estimate.' But clearly, as is conceded, this is largely a semantic distinction. It is obviously the case that true phobia is much less frequent than the spectrum of amorphous fears and anxieties caused by the computer, many of which may be rationally grounded and so outside the province of phobia as a psychiatric condition. Heller and Bower have proposed a fear-type definition of phobia rather than attempting a strict clinical description.

They ask *'What Is Your CPQ?'* (Computer Phobia Quotient), and then invite readers to answer ten questions to discover their degree of phobia. Some of the questions are well rehearsed in the anxiety literature: for example, computers will cause people to lose their jobs; computers are taking over our society; it's getting out of control. Other questions suggest that you have to be a 'mathematical/scientific whiz' to understand computers ('they're just too complicated'), and that only 'strange *computer freaks*' use computers. And sometimes there is a feminist angle, 'There aren't many career opportunities for women in computer-related jobs; Men have more aptitude for programming than women.' If you answer 'Yes' to seven or more of the questions then you are deemed to have a high CPQ. But there are grounds for comfort ('You are not alone. Many intelligent and talented women feel uncomfortable with computers'). If, at the other extreme, you score less than 40 (each 'Yes' rating 10), then 'learning about computers doesn't really present a problem to you'.

The Heller and Bower (1983) book is written for women, so it is worth acknowledging that computer fears and phobias are more likely to be encouraged in women than in men. Most Western cultures give women negative messages about their ability to deal with technology, and this is no less true where the technology is computer-based. It is possible that women have computer fears that are much less common in men (without straying into the nature/nurture debate there is almost certainly a cultural element in this).

We see that most definitions of computer phobia say little about phobia *per se*. There is little said about the phobia stock-in-trade – such as sweating, palpitations, vomiting, sudden dizziness, etc. Most of the computer 'phobia' that is discussed in the literature is legitimate anxiety, sensible worries about the likely impact of computers on jobs, understandable trepidation about having to come to terms with a widespread technological intruder. In a recent book by Peter Large (*The Micro Revolution Revisited*), there is even a reference to the *'computer allergy'* now evident in Japan. If worry about computers is not a *phobia* then it is an *allergy*. In fact it is rarely either but the ready use of such terminology suggests that computers are already seen as disturbing interlopers in human society. It is hard to imagine that this situation will improve.

Phobia at Home

Sometimes the symptoms of computer phobia (however defined) appear in the domestic environment. Here the doubts and anxieties are much the same as elsewhere but they occur in a place that is supposed to be comfortable and supportive. Perhaps a young son or daughter is pressing parents to learn

Basic, to try the keyboard, or at least to 'come and see my new program'. Sarah Kortum (1983), in her engaging series on 'Confessions of a Reformed Computer Phobic' (in *Family Computing*), also goes in for the definition game. In one article she asks the inevitable question: *'Do you suffer from cyberphobia* (fear of computers)?'. I you find yourself repeating certain catch phrases – often in the home but sometimes elsewhere – then you are probably a sufferer. Do *you* find yourself saying: 'I don't *want* to know how to use one', 'I don't have time', 'I'm not the computer type', 'I'm too old', 'It's going to make me obsolete', or 'I'm stupid'. If you find yourself saying such things – to offspring or employer – then perhaps Kortum is right. You *want* to learn how to use a computer but wonder whether you are capable. But don't worry: you'll cope, and 'you won't wake up in the middle of the night and see your home computer running off with the family car – or your wife'.

Sometimes parents are oddly anxious about their offspring's new computer acquisition. The reaction of Janet Hecker, reported by Kortum, when her son introduced a microcomputer into her Florida home was perhaps not all that unusual. She was terrified to touch it: 'I was totally afraid I was going to ruin everything. So I just dusted around it.' She had thought that computers lived in big rooms filled with machinery but now there was one *sitting in her son's bedroom*. In due course Janet Hecker learned to use the computer but first she had to conquer her computer phobia which she described as 'fear of the unknown'. And she felt how many parents have felt: 'I felt like I was being completely passed by . . . I felt like I had been born thirty years too late.' Thre was also the common fear of failure. She could cope with a typewriter or an adding machine but *computers frightened her*. Eventually, after conquering her anxieties, she believes that the micro is the best investment the family has ever made.

Another case reported by Sarah Kortum concerns a certain David Wilson who, at 43 and the manager of a retail store, decided to buy an Apple II microcomputer. On one occasion he ventured to an Apple users' group meeting ('I felt stupid'), not daring to ask questions but hoping to 'absorb osmotically' as much as he could. In the early days he did not know the right questions to ask, and when people tried to help it simply made things worse: 'As soon as they started talking about strings and arrays I just went into very quiet hysteria.'

By his second month with the Apple he had developed 'a growing sense of I'm just not going to be able to hack it'. In fact now the computer – whether seen as a domestic tool or an object essential for business success – had triggered a fear 'that I'm not going to be able to survive or deal or cope with the world that's being created around me. *I* just wasn't adequate.' At one stage he even became superstitious about the machine, feeling that he had to 'sneak up' on it, '*to catch it unawares, so it would work!*' Eventually the computer, a distressing symbol of his incompetence, got covered up with junk mail, later to be 'bundled up' and stuck in the closet. There was, however, a happy ending. Months later, David Wilson received the help he needed, took the computer from the closet and began the learning task all over again – this time with help from a computer science graduate from MIT. Now he is an instructor of more than a dozen computer classes at the Cambridge and Boston centres for adult education. One of his courses is called 'Stalking the Wild Computer', based on his early phobic experiences. This has reassured many of his students who themselves may have deep-seated fears about computers. ('I can usually see it on their faces, all of a sudden this draining of tension! It's very reassuring to them that they're not the only ones who have that fear.') Many of the students will have their own microcomputers at home (possession of a micro is now a condition of computer education in some American colleges), and if they themselves are not fearful, perhaps their parents are sometimes anxious. Computers, we have seen, can generate *phobia, allergy, tension* and *hysteria*: they are potent forces to introduce into the family and other social sectors.

It is common for new owners of home computers to experience some anxiety. In another *Family Computing* article, Cindy Frenkel (1983) describes how a family acquired an Apple II microcomputer. Tony Morris recalls: ' We went from fear of hurting our new equipment, to frustration when we lost our first few programs, and finally to ease. Suddenly all fear of the machine was gone . . . .' Sometimes the fear passes, sometimes it grows. Contact with computers, where successful and leading to human (rather than machine) mastery, is likely to remove anxiety and the growing fear that one cannot cope. But there is more to computers than how one feels about them in the domestic or small-business environment. The number of computer species is already growing at a rapid rate and someone who is not fearful of a spider might well be phobic about a snake.

Phobia at Work

Many of the most serious cases of computer phobia concern anxieties about the computer impact on employment. We have seen that it is not only the possibility of computers replacing people in the workplace – though this is perhaps one of the most devastating consequences of computer encroachment – but also the effects of working *with* computer-based systems that can cause concern. People may wonder if they are really *in control,* and if having a computer as a colleague is not disconcerting then on occasions it can be very frustrating. There is an interesting case reported in the *Human Factors Society Bulletin* (**24**, 8, 1981). An individual managing the implementaton of a new computer system for various police and sheriff departments received a call one day: 'Your terminal is dead. Come get it.' It was found that *the terminal had two bullet holes*! An officer, having been presented with 'Do not understand' once too often, had stepped back and shot it. Most cases of computer phobia – or computer hostility – are less extreme.

We have seen that many computer phobics have what may be seen as rational grounds for their anxiety. They may, for instance, rightly wonder whether they are about to be made redundant by automated systems. But sometimes irrational fears themselves may make an individual a poor employment prospect. We have already referred to Mike Legut counselling phobic cases at the San Francisco Phobia Centre; recently he has been counselling what he calls *cyberphobics.* He comments: 'People who have this phobia really don't like to tell others they are afraid of computers. It could mean their jobs.'

When a company decides to buy a computer-based system for the office or some other environment, there are often the classic phobic reactions of opposition or avoidance ('fight or flight'). A person may leave the company simply because computers are about to be installed, and if the person stays on the premises there may be attempts at sabotage. ('He may do everything to make sure the system won't work.') Again the same old worries are discernible. Users – sometimes high-level managers – may doubt their ability to cope. They may declare that they were never any good at mathematics ('It's too hard'), and may opt out of all decision-making. One case cited by Legut concerned an administrator working in a law firm. She panicked when she found out that the attorneys were about to install a computer in the office. ('All of a sudden she hates her job. This new situation has provoked a flight response.')

Another case concerns a manager at a large business company. Charged with the task of choosing a computer for the firm, he is deliberating delaying, uncertain of how to proceed and anxious not to appear incompetent. And another Legut client, a cured agoraphobic, managed to use her earlier therapy to cope with the prospect of having to work with computers. She is employed as a secretary in California and comments that if she had been told 6 years ago that she was being offered a job using a computer then she would not have taken it: 'I would be afraid of making a mistake, or erasing the program or making the computer self-destruct.' In due course, she learned to cope and bought a Commodore VIC 20 for home use. When she found out that an IBM Personal Computer was arriving at her workplace she was delighted.

Efforts have been made to chart in detail the character of computer phobia in the working situation. In a much discussed article, Harold and Elizabeth Guarnieri (1982) begin by citing the firm, typical of many, that introduced computers in an atmosphere of great optimism, only to find that the anticipated jump in company productivity did not occur. Quite the reverse! After the new system had been operating for 6 months, productivity had declined, clerical morale was at an all-time low, and the computer system was ridiculed. Far from the computer bringing new advantages, staff were reluctant to use it. The managers thought that they had planned the installation well, and they were baffled. What had gone wrong?

Companies are commonly finding that staff are resisting easy-to-use computer-based systems. Clerks are reluctant to move from typewriters to word processors, middle managers wonder whether to trust the computerized innovations, and senior executives are unwilling to use a straightforward keyboard to access vital financial information. The Guarnieri's recommend that information managers recognize *the phenomenon of the Psycho-Computer Syndrome*. It is emphasized that when mechanical systems were first introduced it was thought that perhaps the lever would cause the muscles to atrophy. Today there are analogous suspicions about the computer, the 'lever of the mind'. Some employees seem to believe that the mind will cease to function if computers are used, and others doubt that computers can be consistently accurate and efficient.

One company introduced a computer terminal into their purchasing department, choosing the most competent clerk in the office to operate it. In fact she had not been prepared for the change, and had formerly acquired the belief that computers necessarily eliminate jobs – so she would be the first casualty! When pressed to use the terminal, *she vomited all over the new equipment!* To avoid such events, managements are advised to educate staff in good time, preparing them well in advance for any changes that will affect their working routines. In this context the Psycho-Computer Syndrome is recognized as exhibiting an eight-stage motivational pattern that is always evident during the training of a first-time user. The Guarnieri's indentify the eight stages that traditional office workers go through in their transition to members of a computerized office:

1. There are first *general feelings of emotional and intellectual insecurity*. Job definitions are changed so that workers can adjust to unfamiliar practices and techniques. In essence, the worker is asked 'to evolve almost instantaneously . . .'. There is bound to be a sense of anxiety, a 'gnawing fear that he may not be able to learn the new skills as quickly as he should'.

2. *Ego-status disintegration* is the next discernible condition to emerge, and it is close connected with the types of feelings generated in Stage 1. Again the worker may worry about acquiring the necessary skills and discipline. If Stage 2 is not negotiated satisfactorily then Stage 3 will be entered with feelings of hostility.

3. *Hostility/challenge* is now detectable. If the worker has coped with Stage 2, then the computer will begin to be seen as a challenge. It will be realised that other people have had problems, and that perhaps there are benefits in computers after all. Less successful workers, feeling unsafe, will exhibit antagonism. (The Guarnieri's comment: 'No doubt you have heard of *beverages dumped into the electronics; magnets run across storage media; and metal filings, cigarette butts and water inside computer enclosures. We have also seen wire cut'*.) Managements should do all they can to minimise any unwelcome events in Stage 3. Above all, they should involve the workers, sharing decision-making, and

indicating the benefits that the new equipment will bring.
4. There is next a *search for equilibrium*, the first sign that
training can begin. Here there is an element of resignation.
The worker may feel that, in order to protect his job, he
must go along with the management plans. If he is not
interested in job security then group acceptance may be an
important motivating influence. In any event, he is ready
to move to Stage 5. If the equilibrium is *not* reached during
Stage 4 then the worker may regress to an earlier stage, and
the career development of that individual – if he stays in
employment – may be a protracted affair.
5. Here the worker is interested in the *formation of a support
group*, a group that shares his point of view. This may be
seen as an essentially social reaction. The way in which the
worker has negotiated Stage 4 will determine the character
of the support group that is regarded as convivial. If the
person is still hostile then he will naturally seek a group
that is antipathetic to the changes envisaged by
management.
6. At this stage there are the *first significant learning successes*, a real breakthrough. Positive experience at this stage
will act as a catalyst for movement towards Stage 7.
7. Here we have *ego-status integration*, the reversal of what
tended to happen at Stage 2. Now the worker is moving
towards a position of acceptance. He is inclined to think
that the skills and discipline required in the new situation
are achievable. He is likely by now to have achieved some
concrete successes and is motivated to build on them ('He
seems to have one "Ah-ha, so that's what it means!"
experience after another'). Stage 7 'may represent his most
exhilarating moments'. Here management can be con-
fident that an acceptable pattern will emerge – 'you will
guide your staff very little if at all'. Management, at this
stage, will be 'observer and validator'.
8. By now *equilibrium* has been established, there is a new
office routine. Ideally, at this stage, the computer has
become an ally. The worker has steadied himself and made
a satisfactory shift to new routines. He has seen the benefits of the new equipment and has evolved into an information worker.

It is not suggested that the scheme, as laid out, is necessarily a
formula for success. Many workers, we may assume, will fall by

the wayside – if only because many managers will not have the necessary insight and sensitivity to the workers' emotional and psychological problems. For our purposes the whole scheme is replete with phobic possibilities. It is acknowledged, for example, that hostility and resentment are to expected, that workers may be driven into recalcitrance and antagonism: an impulse to sabotage is, seemingly, not at all surprising. Nor does the working out of the Psycho-Computer Syndrome necessarily imply that competent managements can avoid these sorts of undesirable consequences. For the situation is complex. The person's motivational needs are important, as is the sensitivity of management, the quality of the training, and the reliability and complexity of the system. There are many points at which the evolution from office worker to information worker can be distorted or even totally arrested. There is no harm in a *counsel of perfection* unless it is assumed to be an infallible formula for success.

We can highlight some of the reactions of workers to the introduction of computer-based systems, as shown in the brief case studies presented by Harold and Elizabeth Guarnieri:

1. One worker, fearful of unemployment, vomited over her terminal.
2. Another worker, formerly relaxed and friendly with two other clerks, began to dissociate herself from them and to find fault. They, in turn, isolated her more and more.
3. A cost accounting clerk experienced a direct loss of status and felt that there was no control over the system. She only regained her lost ego-status when the management agreed to delay the implementation of the system.
4. Managers in distribution and cost accounting were disturbed by discrepancies in system outputs. A clerk researched the situation and uncovered a thief. It was also found that different systems were interpreting the same data differently.

Managements are often exhorted not to see staff reactions as problems but as indications of actions to be taken. But in many cases the implicit faith – that good management can remove all the causes of anxiety – is at best naive and at worst totally groundless. The presentation (in Guarnieri and Guarnieri, 1982) of the Psycho-Computer Syndrome says nothing about redundancy, nothing about the inevitable job deskilling in some areas, nothing about systems that grow too complex for real comprehension. The sources of fear and phobia in the workplace cannot be eliminated totally by enlightened training and sensitive management. Companies are profit-oriented rather than people-oriented: phobias, by definition, have irrational roots, but a real spectrum of legitimate fears may follow a calm and rational assessment of the likely impact of computer systems in one job area after another. And managers and executives should not feel too complacent about this: already efforts are being made to build detailed commercial planning and business judgement into computer software.

We see a spectrum of factors that can generate legitimate anxiety in workers threatened by computerization. The danger to employment is no myth (see chapter 3), nor is the idea that automation can further entrench already powerful groupings in company hierarchies. Management layers controlling the decisions on automation are likely to extend their dominance over other company sectors: to control company information is to establish a formidable power base. And it is hard to see how the mass of ordinary workers can benefit in this scenario. We can imagine many ways in which this situation is ripe for fear and phobia.

The journal *Computerworld* carried a number of pieces by Jack Stone and Joanne Barker, in a series entitled 'DPers and the Psychocomputer Syndrome', responding to the Guarnieri article. First (Stone and Barker, 1983a), they question the Weinberg suggestion that 'as many as 30% of our population are cyberphobiacs': as we have seen, this rapidly becomes a semantic matter. One possibility was that Weinberg was suggesting that the new users were neurotic *before* they encountered computers, the later automation programmes simply intensifying their problems. If people already have a stack of troublesome personal and social pressures, the prospect of having to cope with computers may be the last straw – thoughts of having to work with computing machinery may 'only accentuate hostile attitudes'. In such circumstances, systems managers would have to become 'pseudopsychiatrics' in order to implement new computer systems – 'Is a DPer the kind of person you want to treat your neurosis?'

Next (Stone and Barker, 1983b) it is suggested that the Guarnieri article should have carried a large label bearing the words:

Warning!! Computer Industry Leaders Have Determined
That Mishandling Cyberphobiac Users Is Injurious to An
Organisation's Health

And again the question is asked: is the typical DP manager
really equipped, without intensive training and experience in
psychology, to recognize such things as 'ego-status disintegration', the 'search for equilibrium', and 'ego-status integration'? Should DP managers be expected to function as prac-
tising psychologists? Stone and Barker know the answer to such
questions – 'No!' Yet it is obvious that there is a powerful
psychological component in most good-management activity.

But are the Guarnieri's also exaggerating the problem – we
may get the impression *'that there are an awful lot of nuts running
loose in user departments . . . Balderdash!'* Of course, Stone and
Barker concede that people have their problems. It is understandable that there should be *'valid and natural concerns, fears and
apprehensions about automation'* – but it is inaccurate and unfair
to attribute incapacitating phobias to a large part of the user
population.

It may also be the case (Stone and Barker, 1983c) that the bulk
of the fears and apprehensions experienced by new users would
also be felt by perfectly normal people about to face a totally new
working situation. There are bound to be a few true cyberphobiacs with irrational responses and the tendency to suffer
intolerable pressures when they hear that 'the machines are
coming'. At the same time we are urged to remember that
another limited population, without computer experience, is
liable to greet new terminals with enthusiasm and joy. Moreover, we should also consider whether the DPers, likely to
prefer interaction with computers to intercourse with people,
should be dubbed *'anthrophobic'*. A mere preference, Stone and
Barker imply, should not be equated with a psychiatric condition. DPers may have their doubts, concerns and anxieties
about the competence of terminal operators, about whether the
system will ever be functioning as the designers proposed, and
about the secret machinations of management (ever prepared to
blame the data processing department for any systems failures).
Yet the mentalities of DPers are seldom discussed in psychiatric
terms. (But is this strictly true? Is it not the case that hackers are
often dubbed *'obsessive'*, *'compulsive'*, etc? Are they not
sometimes seen as *'paranoic'* when managements decide to cut

the DP investment levels? It may be, as we have suggested already, that computers have the peculiar capacity to generate *various* mental states in human beings, some of which states may be less than healthy.)

It is also questionable (Stone and Barker, 1983d) whether it is wise to tell the training manager to expect that 'a third of the class may be so cyberphobiac as to thrust their fists through the display tubes'. If a person displays illness symptoms – if the person is a 'true cyberphobiac' – then that person should be released from the office and directed to a medical professional. But the typical new employee should be expected to conquer the normal apprehensions during training and to learn to cope with the computers.

Finally (Stone and Barker, 1983c) Stone and Barker report contact with one true cyberphobiac. A brief question-and-answer sequence reveals something of the mental turmoil of the woman in question. She began by having trouble with the whole range of office products, with the computer 'the absolute worst'. She was able to cope with cars and other personal machines but the computer-based machines in business were perceived as immensely threatening. She suffers when she hears that a new machine is coming to the office – 'I find myself panic-stricken and seriously afflicted by a continuing stream of anxieties and insecurities.' And again the problem is linked to a perceived incompetence in mathematics and science: just as school and college tests would always threaten to reveal her 'stupidity' to teachers, so new office machines would allow the boss to find out about her ('and demote me or even fire me').

The woman found that a host of emotional imbalances were triggered off whenever there was a prospect of a computer arriving at the office. Her mind would race along from mania (an 'even thrilling kind of euphoria') to sudden depression, whereupon she would feel paranoid pressure. She had a serious attack when due to attend for computer training, and remembered little except taking home the computer manual to read it before the class was due to start. Then she woke up next day in the psychiatric ward of a hospital to find that she had suffered a nervous breakdown. She returned to work after a month and gradually came to terms with computers ('although I'll never embrace the machine with tender, loving care, I'm sort of looking forward to learning more about it'). In her view the problems could have been avoided if management had handled the situation differently: she had needed assurance about time off for training and that she would not be graded during the process.

We may speculate on the precise nature of this woman's condition. It is not uncommon for phobia to be associated with other unhealthy mental states, and it might have been useful to know whether the woman was also phobic about other items or events. In such instances it is hard to see how DP managers can be expected to adopt therapeutic tactics that may require specialist psychiatric knowledge. A poor manager may encourage a fear to develop into a phobia, but if a department is presented with a new employee already afflicted with various psychiatric complaints – the woman had been treated for manic-depression – then the problems associated with anxiety and apprehension are likely to be magnified.

In fact various attempts have been made to investigate the computer-specialist mentality. Woodruff (1980), for instance, asks: 'Data Processing People – *Are They Really Different?*'. He carried out personality profiles of 202 data-processing (DP) personnel, and comparisons were made of the DP males and females with their general population counterparts. In summary, the DP males and females were found to have remarkably similar personality profiles. The DP males were found to have high needs for *endurance, achievement, cognitive structure* and *harm-avoidance*; low needs for *aggression* and *social recognition*. Similarly, the DP females possess high needs for *endurance, cognitive structure* and *achievement*; a low need for *affiliation*.

What is there in this that we may imagine to be relevant to computer fears and phobias? Very little. There is the suggestion that the men are more interested than are the women in 'harm-avoidance'. Hence Woodruff observes that the greatest deviation in personality between males and females 'occurs with the need for harm-avoidance which, it would seem, is applicable hopefully to a limited number of DP work environments'. We would expect harm-avoidance to be causally and statistically linked with fear or anxiety, which suggests that men are more likely than women to be fearful in the computer environment. And the picture can be rounded out.

The men are, seemingly, low on aggression and the need for social recognition. This suggests a certain diffidence, a propensity to adopt a 'laid back' attitude to life. Taken with the harm-avoidance ratings, the male DP specialists may be interested in neutralizing anxiety by not courting trouble. The picture that emerges is one of slightly apprehensive males seeking solace in the unreal social world of the computer. If such males *are* more anxious, and so more prone to fears and phobias than are their female counterparts, then this shows an interesting reversal of the situation in the population at large: it is well known that, for the full range of phobia, there are many more female sufferers than males.

It is clear that computers can generate a range of anxieties in the working situation, and that some of these anxieties will assume phobic dimensions in particular personalities. We will see that many of the circumstances of the worker in the computer environment involve bad environmental conditions, undue stress, heightened psychological tension, etc. It is not difficult to see why the manufacture, use and social impact of computers should cause apprehension in most human societies.

The Answer

What is the answer to computer phobia at home and in the workplace. Contact between people and computers is supposed to be helpful, but it can be counterproductive. If people *understand*, they can usually cope more effectively – so training, initiation, discussions, joint decision-making in the firm, etc. are all valuable. There are educators (for example, Diane Resick and José Gutierrez at the San Francisco State University) who conduct courses bearing such titles as 'Computers *without fear*' and 'Math *without fear*'. But the problem is immense. Computers do not only generate apprehension for a few simple reasons: the threat they pose is multifaceted, multidimensional.

It is even possible to argue that there are legitimate grounds for anxiety that have not yet been perceived by most citizens in the advanced world. Today many people, mostly ignorant about computers, have a general unease about certain aspects of technological innovation. They like their video recorders but may be concerned about nuclear power or whether 'computers will take over the world'. If already people have a general apprehension about intelligent machines, without having any detailed knowledge about computer capabilities, how will they feel when they realize that even the experts do not fully understand the new generation of machines, and that it is to the caprice of such incomprehensible systems that we are consigning judgements on nuclear war? (We consider these points in more detail in later chapters.) First it is worth highlighting some of the consequences of working in the computer environment.

The Hazards at Work

For computer workers in the developed countries the problems tend to start with 'finished' systems, i.e. with systems that are already configured. For example, there may be problems concerning stress or ergonomics. Sometimes there is focus on the need to build a system from the chip level upwards, but this is usually left to manufacturers: people working to *implement* systems are usually concerned with getting the total complex of hardware and software 'up and running'. In general, little attention is given to the basic fabrication activities upon which the whole edifice of the computer industry depends; namely, the making of integrated circuits ('chips') and the related assembly of basic computer components.

Today, with a worldwide shortage of silicon chips, many types of components are manufactured in the developed countries. However, for a variety of economic and political reasons, a large proportion of chip manufacture is conducted in the Third World – often in appalling working conditions that can result in damaged eyes, sickness and other ailments.

Semiconductor electronics is one of the fastest-growing industry sectors in Southeast Asia. Upwards of 300,000 women are currently assembling the miniscule components that are required by products ranging from digital watches to the vast supercomputers produced by such companies as Cray and Cyber. The large semiconductor companies have evolved a whole spectrum of policies and measures to maintain the various Third World workforces in conditions of low-paid subservience. For example, personnel policies have been designed to develop sexist attitudes among the predominantly female employees on the assembly lines: organized recreational activities focus on sewing classes, shoe sales, singing competitions and beauty contests. Company magazines project an endless stream of images of women as sex objects and passive consumers. Grossman (1979) has emphasized the main purpose of such policies: *'the guiding principle behind all the clever games becomes suddenly visible: control'*.

In many Third World factories, workers are prohibited from talking, discipline is strict, and there are few breaks in the working day (workers at the Fairchild factory in Indonesia have reported being allowed only a 15-minute lunch break in the 8-hour day shift). Workers are encouraged to identify with the fortunes of the company, and not to join trade unions ('Intel doesn't believe in unions'). A Californian semiconductor executive has attacked unions for making it more difficult for firms to lay off workers. What we see is the systematic exploitation of cheap labour in conditions of high unemployment: AMD-Philippines, for example, reported as many as 500 applicants a week for 50 jobs. Today low-cost labour is producing silicon chips in such countries as Taiwan, South Korea, Malaysia, Thailand, the Philippines and Hong Kong.

In such places strenuous efforts are made to suppress worker protests about rates of pay or working conditions. Police and government officials will quickly descend on a plant when a protest begins, with strikes generally prohibited in 'vital' industries (usually encompassing foreign-owned manufacturing plants). It is impossible to consider the impact of chip manufacture without paying some attention to political and social factors. In the Philippines, for example, Presidential Decree 148 (1972) reduced the level of maternity benefits to make it more profitable for large companies to employ women workers, often in unhealthy environments.

Electronics workers in the factories are commonly afflicted by toxic chemicals and eye ailments, yet companies appear reluctant to inform employees of possible health hazards (Grossman: *'management-run health and safety committees actually divert attention from these problems'*). Three years after the first electronics plant opened in Penang in 1972, nearly half the workers complained of deteriorating eyesight and frequent headaches, the inevitable consequence of excessive microscope work; and a majority of Hong Kong electronics workers over the age of 25 are forced to wear glasses.

There is often inadequate control over the storing and use of toxic chemicals in the factories. Such chemicals, often giving off powerful fumes and suspected of being carcinogenic, include TOE, xylane and MEK, dangerous acids and solvents employed extensively throughout the manufacturing process.

Components are often manually dipped into acids: burns, dizziness, nausea and even lost fingers may result. And it is suggested that the possible carcinogenic effects of the chemicals will not be known before several years have elapsed and it is too late to take effective protective action. The comfortable programmers, systems analysts and DP managers in the developed countries do not always realise the human price paid for fancy computer installations. And these types of problems are not confined to the underdeveloped world.

In a remarkable article, 'Life on the Line', Kathy Chin (writing in *Infoworld*, 14 May 1984) describes the conditions of workers in Silicon Valley, California. One task is to put wires into circuit boards – 'The most taxing challenge is trying to think of something to think about after two hours of mindless routine. How can people do this for years on end?' Pay is low and there are health problems. ('Sometimes my eyes get so tired, they get red every time I go home.') Many of the workers are Third World immigrants – so sometimes the factories can be seen as an Asian subculture, subject to the privations that characterize the factories in such countries as Thailand and South Korea. For example, in 1984 Silicon Valley workers could earn as little as $3.50 an hour. And in such circumstances there is little job security.

As in the factories of the Third World, the Californian workers are often expected to work with hazardous chemicals. For example, a 1984 lawsuit focused on a 35-year-old woman who died of scleroderma, a disorder of connective tissue. According to her attorney: 'This became a progressive skin disease that resulted from the chemical situation on the job.' Another worker recalled how, in one Californian factory, asbestos was 'falling down from the ceiling like snow'. Yet other workers have complained about acid fumes, the resulting poor health, and totally inadequate protection in the working environment. With the fabrication requirements for acids, solvents and other dangerous chemicals, the computer industry has sired a whole new spectrum of hazard for worker and citizen alike. Environmental pollution is not caused only by the old traditional industries.

The stress and health risks encountered by Asian and Californian workers is one element in the situation, the problems encountered by computer employees working with installed systems quite another. We do not expect most computer professionals to encounter carcinogenic chemicals, but they have their own sources of stress and aggravation.

Computer operators, programmers and systems analysts find themselves in difficulties because of poor job scheduling and inconsiderate project management. These were possible reasons for the difficulties laid out by Ben Woolley (1982): he presents some of the consequences of stress and boredom in computer workers. These various unfortunate consequences are together dubbed the 'Shoestring Syndrome', a multifaceted condition that afflicts people in different ways. For example, a programmer is quoted on the state of one of his colleagues:

> The overworked employee had seemingly cracked. An operator had found the conversion programmer babbling, crying and generally incoherent. His hands were shaking uncontrollably, so much so that when he placed his hands under a desk, the whole thing shook.

A DP manager talks of depression: first he worked under tremendous pressure, then there was a lull, and finally he felt unable to accept any work at all. Tracy Kidder (1982), talking about the frantic development of Data General's first 32-bit minicomputer, records the impact of work pressure on computer designers: 'I've had difficulty forming sentences lately. In the middle of a story my mind will go blank. Pieces of your life get dribbled away.' And one of the project members complained of a tiredness that 'going home won't solve'. Another programmer, cited by Woolley, declared himself 'broken, health-wise' after a stint with a systems house. Woolley comments ironically: 'Maybe the demon in the black box has a mind of its own, and is reaping revenge for all the insult we rain on it. Man's attempts to recreate his brain seem to be backfiring.'

The Shoestring Syndrome has already been dubbed an allergic reaction. It is well known that certain people can be allergic to man-made objects; for example, those made of plastic. There is no reason why computer workers should not have their quota of allergic reaction, though their allergies would normally relate to washing powders and pollen spores. Dr Cedrid Wilson (1982), commenting on the Shoestring Syndrome, suggests that it may be linked to Total Allergy Syndrome (TAS), produced in a patient through sensitivity to a wide range of foreign proteins and other chemicals in the environment. Stress may be seen as a result of the allergic reaction, and such stress may become more widespread with the spread of computers into the home and elsewhere. Wilson, a consultant physician, suggests that high concentrations of chemical allergens and the lengthy duration of pressure in the computer room may bring on signs of the Shoestring Syndrome: 'It must be recognised that the challenge produced in the computer room on the computer operators is able to cause a significant work hazard as a result of which serious degeneration in physical and mental function may occur.'

It is at least possible that a proportion of the DP-induced stress found in employees is associated with allergic reactions, as it is also associated with management pressure, excessive consumption of alcohol and other drugs, paranoia, and associated fears and phobias. In any event, whatever the explanation of stress conditions in particular individuals, it is clear that their incidence is increasing in computer workers.

At a 1983 conference on performance management, sponsored by Applied Computer Research, Dr Thomas McDonald discussed the incidence of DP-related stress. This condition is currently limited largely to full-time computing professionals, but as computers spread so will the stress that they engender, until it is found in almost every walk of life. In his keynote address McDonald predicted that society as a whole will come to have as much experience of DP-caused stress as DP managers have at present.

It is emphasized that little is currently known about how computing effects people, but a study carried out by the National Institute of Occupational Safety and Health found evidence to suggest that:

> Among computer professionals annual job turnover ranges from 25% to 40%.

> The home life of nearly one in every seven computing specialists is adversely affected by information systems work.

> Work in data processing ranks 12th in the list of the world's 115 most stressful occupations.

There are many sources of stress in computing work (McDonald: 'There's a ton of stress in DP'), and much of this stems from the consequences of systems failure. Computers are now so important to successful company operation that a DP failure can incur immense dislocation and inconvenience. The computer staff at the heart of the problem when it occurs are made to think that they are solely responsible – when in fact the blame may lie elsewhere (for example, with senior managements denying the investment funds necessary for smooth operation). Conversely, DP staff are usually 'out of sight, out of mind' when things are tripping along smoothly.

McDonald also confirmed that non-technical and other individuals often fear computers and resist their introduction into the workplace (Beeler, 1983). Corporate executives may worry about automation because their ignorance may make them look stupid in the eyes of their subordinates. Other staff may, quite reasonably, worry about job security, or about the disruption of informal personnel networks. Managements need to take active steps to promote a good image of computers, if only to counter 'the endless chorus of user complaints'. In such circumstances it is inevitable that computers will tend to be badly perceived, and that stress levels will increase – leading not only to illness and high staff turnover, but to such things as child neglect and marital breakdown (see chapter 5).

It has recently emerged (*Computing*, 15 March 1984) that the divorce rate in Silicon Valley is 33 per cent higher than the US national average. The penalties of success in this competitive environment are divorce, drug abuse, alcoholism and – to use a Valley buzz-word – 'burn-out'. Jean Hollands, a leading expert on *silicon stress* and founder of the Good Life Clinic in Mountainview, now heads a staff of 25 to provide therapy for more than 3000 couples. She observes that there are more marital problems and stress in the computer industry than in any other walk of life. ('I counsel in a high-stress world where wives all too often find themselves competing with hardware and software for their husbands' affections.')

Today there are around 162,000 people working in Silicon Valley (including an estimated 15,000 dollar millionaires) but many are under intolerable pressures that lead to physical and mental illness. Professor Cary Cooper, of the Department of Management Sciences at the University of Manchester Institute of Science and Technology (UMIST), has suggested that what is happening in Silicon Valley is symptomatic of developments in the computer industry all over the world (*Computer Talk*, 19 March 1984). Cooper, an author of several books on stress (including *Executive Families Under Stress, The Stress Check*), suggests that even individuals employed in 'safe' companies like IBM are not cushioned from the stress factors. The computer industry, promoted as easing man's lot, has at least added another high-stress industry to those that already exist.

Many of these factors relate to systems design, the *ergonomic* considerations that are relevant to how well individuals can cope with a computer environment. There is a massive literature of *ergonomics, human-factors engineering, design for health and safety,* and it is increasingly being recognized that there is a psychological dimension to these considerations (thus, Meilach, 1983, for example, observes: 'Phobias, stress and depression are being chronicled . . .'). Even the decision to buy a home computer can, as we have seen, be fraught with problems; and the difficulties in the working situation are more complicated. Individual employees are more constrained, having little option but to obey management directives; the managers and executives have their own problems. A vice president at a Dallas bank has been quoted as saying: 'We find it easier to cure computer phobia among our executives if we train them at centres away from the office . . . We have to provide a private place for them to conquer their fears, overcome their timidity and learn to communicate in the computerised office.' Again it is emphasized that high-ranking individuals find it demeaning to betray their ignorance in front of subordinates.

The psychologist, Dr Thomas McDonald, has constructed a Computer Stress Test to ascertain some of the pressures to which computer staff are subjected. The individuals are asked to answer yes or no to various questions, including:

> I get blamed if data vanishes.
>
> I sometimes feel inadequate around computers.
>
> I get frustrated when my computer commands are rejected.
>
> Sometimes I feel like hitting my computer.
>
> Sometimes I think of sabotaging a program.
>
> People expect me to be perfect.

The computer specialist, who may lack assertiveness and be weak on relationship skills, may swallow the pressure – until the point when anxiety and depression take over. Here there may be high rates of absenteeism and high levels of staff mobility from one company to another. And the psychological problems have a number of physical counterparts which have been the traditional concern of the ergonomics experts.

Great effort has been put into designing terminals so that eyestrain, backache and other undesirable consequences are avoided. It has been claimed that electromagnetic radiation from terminal screens can cause cataracts and even birth defects (see, for example the report by Kirchner, 1984). It is well known that excessive terminal use can cause dizziness, nausea and disorientation; and that epileptics, alcoholics and people on Valium may be adversely affected by prolonged contact with terminal screens. Even where the more extreme claims – for example, of baby deformity or spontaneous abortion – are discounted, there is often manufacturer and management recognition that contact with terminals should be limited to relatively short time durations. Today some officially endorsed recommendations now specify that terminals should not be used continuously for more than 2 hours, and that there should not be more than two of these sessions per working day.

Moreover, it is often declared that the state of ergonomic design leaves much to be desired. The computer-terminal operator is forced to adapt to an environment which represents a negation of the capabilities of the human hands and which is seen by the eyes as *a source of perceived danger*. 'The first element tends to make the operator a slave; the second a hunted animal'. If this is only partly true it is easy to see why there is resistance to technological innovation in the office environment and elsewhere.

We see a working environment for computer staff that is fraught with hazard, and which is likely to engender a disturbing spectrum of apprehension, anxiety, fear and phobia. The threats, we have seen, vary according to the nature of the working environment, but there are common elements. Most computer employees are subject to directives with which they may or may not feel at ease. This is an inevitable part of the employment scene, but one that is magnified and shaped in various ways by the exigencies of the computing phenomenon. The sheer pace of development in the computer industry has generated a rapidly changing employment environment, full of pressure, uncertainty and new required modes of behaviour. We do not yet know what the full consequences will be for human psychology. There are, however, plenty of clues.

Other Sources of Threat

Apart from the more obvious domestic and workplace sources of computer fear and phobia, we have already hinted at various other ways in which new technology may generate anxiety and apprehension. Computers may be variously depicted as repressive tools, devices of authoritarian government, a threat to civil liberties, a dynamic factor in class war, a divisive element exacerbating the tensions between the poor and rich nations of the world. All this, and more, can be argued (some of these points are considered later). For it is the powerful flexibility of the computer that makes it such a potent social factor.

Many observers like to believe that the computer is *simply* a tool, taking on the character and objectives of its users. But this is far too passive a metaphor. There can be little doubt that the computer is also a shaper of attitudes: it affects psychological disposition, self-image, expectations, beliefs, motivations. Through its influence on modern cognitive psychology, the computer has a philosophical impact, impinging equally on the religious and humanist views of man. The truly *intelligent* machine is more than a *mere* machine, a *mere* tool. And it is from this circumstance that a unique spectrum of computer-generated threats derives.

2

The Machine Threat

Preamble

Computer fears and phobias do not spring into existence in a cultural vacuum. Every human response – positive or negative – is the result of a complex interaction between incoming information on the one hand and individual expectation on the other. We all *mediate* the information we receive, filtering this and savouring that, weighting the items of information according to our own scale of values. Information about new technology is grist to this discriminating mill: we individually perceive the pace of change and then react according to our prior conditioning. Where many people respond in a broadly similar fashion we are entitled to talk about a political movement, a moral crusade, social consensus, a cultural force, a broad church, public prejudice, mass hysteria.

Historically there have been many attitudes to technology in general, and these are well reflected in art and literature, philosophy and film. Overall there is a peculiar ambivalence, as if technology stirs conflicting elements in human consciousness. Man is curious, restless, thrusting; but also fearful, insecure, conservative. Perhaps both sides of human nature are essential to the survival of *homo sapiens* as a biological species. But where technology can stimulate exciting new possibilities in thoughts and activity, it can also undermine comfortable modes of existence and shatter cherished beliefs. The computer is disturbing in this sense, perhaps to a greater degree than all other artefacts. But how it is regarded is also deeply affected by man's perennial but shifting attitudes to the Machine.

We will see that attitudes over the centuries have helped to shape our image of computers: we have been conditioned by a long acquaintance with science and technology to try to slot intelligent machines into convenient pigeon-holes – but computers do not always fit, and this is one of the sources of our anxiety. In recent years, with the expanding power of technology, there have been many attempts to discover public attitudes to machines and technology in general and individual artefacts (for example, computers) in particular. We can ask people in straw polls or carefully contrived surveys. We can evaluate the results according to this or that statistical theory. Or we can survey the outpourings of literate cultures to assess the prevailing mood. William Davenport (1970), for example, has sampled literary and artistic material to reveal attitudes to the Machine and Technology. Essentially he looks at post-war literature and art, remarking that the statements on the Machine are much the same as they were a hundred years ago, but there is a difference, crucial for our purposes. The tone *'is a bit shriller, more fearful, almost despairing at times'* (my italics).

It is inevitable that attitudes to computers are influenced by general attitudes to technology, with the corollary that moods evoked uniquely by computers will feed back to influence opinions on technology in general. Computing is a subclass of science and technology: any unease that attaches to the broad sweep of technological change will influence our views on any particular group of advanced machines.

Davenport produced three, rather obvious, categories to elicit our attitudes to the Machine and Technology, as shown by post-war art and literature. *What is significant is how frequent are the 'negative' observations.* In Category I are the *Positive or Friendly Statements*. These, partly overlapping, number sixteen; and they variously propose that the Machine is sublime, a beautiful object, a tool for God's purposes, a means to abundance and a moral reawakening. The *Equivocal, Ambivalent or Questioning Statements* in Category II, numbering seventeen, see the Machine producing both awe and fear: perhaps the Machine has great potential, but can we be sure that man will stay in charge? And in Category III, devoted to *Essentially Negative or Unfriendly Statements*, there are no less than thirty-nine items.

Many of these are familiar complaints. The Machine depersonalizes human beings, spoils the beauty of nature, and leads to spiritual, moral and imaginative loss. The Machine will replace thought, muscle and emotion, will bring unemployment, and may extinguish all human life. The Machine is a danger to creativity, encouraging passive amusement; it generates a servitude to a new priesthood, with the hold of Technology as alarming as that of religious bigotry or serfdom. Technology dehumanizes by evading surprise, hazard, grace, chance, unexpected choices. Imagination dies and boredom is the result; participation, a real human need, is discouraged; and people become frustrated, mindless, lacking wonder and purpose.

In these observations there are gloom, pessimism and despair. The Machine, we are told, will rob people of their humanity, undermining purpose, and obscuring all truths that cannot be easily quantified and laid up in computer memories. We are being progressively separated from our biological roots, forced to live in stressful and unnatural ways. This is a powerful indictment. Does it gain weight by contemplation of the computer in particular? Can the computer evade the multiple charges levelled by artists and writers at the broad spectrum of technological development?

One familiar charge against technology is that it is responsible for pollution of the environment. Here we tend to think of smoke stacks, chemical plants, oil spillages and radioactive leaks. We rarely think that computers have much to contribute in this area. Yet we have already encountered the toxic and (possibly) carcinogenic substances involved in the manufacture of silicon chips: there is more to the computer than a clean antiseptic environment with expensive air-conditioning.

Already there have been warnings by the influential Royal Commission on Environmental Pollutions concerning the harmful effects of new technology. In its tenth report on environmental pollution, called *Tackling Pollution – Experience and Prospects*, published early in 1984, the Commission suggests that the Environment Department should adopt a long-term strategy to ensure that no new 'time bombs are set'. One of these time bombs is chemical pollution, sometimes caused by exotic chemicals used by the Silicon Valley manufacturers in California. Reports have appeared in the US press describing pollution caused by seepages from the large vats of chemicals used in the making of silicon chips. The Commission recommends that the Department of the Environment (DoE) should 'give high priority to further research on the potentially polluting effects of electronics and other technologically advanced industries'. We may see it as highly significant that many computer manufacturers have set up business in 'green field' sites – where, in the UK, planning controls have been deliberately relaxed as a far-reaching political decision. And it is further stressed that the pollution controls should apply in what have been dubbed the 'Enterprise Zones', as they apply elsewhere. This is seen as a matter of some urgency, 'particularly since many of the smaller firms may lack the experience and technology to cope with the wastes they generate.' (At the time of writing, June 1984, the environment Minister Patrick Jenkin had still to decide whether to act on any of the Commission's recommendations.)

The pollution question is one of many that troubles the general public and specialist alike. Technology, we all know, is not only polluting the atmosphere and the seas, spreading radiation, corrupting our minds through the mass media, destroying the forests, exterminating animal and plant species, and adulterating our food – technology is also expanding the state's control over the individual, planning to further swell the legions of the unemployed, and plotting the total destruction of human society. We should not be surprised, in such circumstances, that people feel uneasy about technology. Even after the great UK propaganda effort of IT82, a MORI poll revealed that only 35 per cent of the population held favourable views of Information Technology, the spectrum of technological developments that rely upon the computer. (A separate survey of business attitudes revealed that 58 per cent of the respondents thought that information technology would produce further unemployment.)

What we see is a mix of attitudes to technology and the machine. A peculiar fatalism about the course of technological development co-exists with a committed enthusiasm on the part of one minority and a deep suspicion and resentment on the part of another, perhaps larger, minority. The machine is generally perceived as bringing benefits – but at a price. And some mechanophobics suspect that the price will become extortionate in the years ahead.

From Myth to the Modern Age

In the Western world the Greeks were perhaps the first people to reflect on the role of the machine in human society. In imagination and art they fabricated their deities to take care of wisdom and love and war and the business of everyday living. And they did not neglect to contrive a god of the mechanical arts. He had other interests and duties as well.

Hephaestus (the name derived from the Greek words for 'hearth' and 'to kindle') was often seen as the personification of terrestial fire: he knew about volcanoes and the furnace, and in such a guise could appear as the divine blacksmith, the artisan-god, the deity who set about teaching man all the mechanical arts. And it was Hephaestus who built twenty tripods which 'run by themselves to a meeting of the gods and amaze the company by running home again' (*Iliad*, Book XVIII); and who manufactured the giant Talus out of brass, to guard Crete by crushing intruders against his heated body.

But there was one singular feature about Hephaestus. Alone among the other Immortals, Hephaestus had a twisted frame: where all the other gods were distinguished by the perfect symmetry and beauty of their perfect bodies, Hephaestus was lame in both legs and his feet were twisted. A dislocated hip caused him to stumble further, and when he walked among the gods his ungainly movements were said to arouse the 'unquenchable laughter of the Immortals'. But why should this be so? Why should Hephaestus, god of the mechanical arts, his skills often required by the deities, be cast in the Greek imagination as a cripple? His infirmities were not the result of an accident. He was lame from birth: Homer records that Hera, ashamed of the ugliness of her son, tried to hide him from sight 'because he was lame'.

Hephaestus was immensely skilled. He fashioned the palaces on Olympus, the throne and sceptre of Zeus, the winged chariot of Helios, Demeter's sickle, the armour of Achilles, Ariadne's diadem, and countless other symbols and artefacts. With such talent and skill, gifts needed by the gods, why did the perceptive Greeks render Hephaestus lame? There have been fanciful explanations: for example, his twisted limbs were supposed to resemble the shaft of lightning. And there is another notion – that the Greeks, with all their uncommon insight, saw through to the dark side of technology, perceived that the mechanical arts are in some sense alien to man's nature – *so only a truly misshapen creature could bring technology into the world*. The other gods, with their perfect bodies and divine looks, gave man wisdom, music, love, and all the glories of the natural world. Hephaestus, the brilliantly accomplished cripple, brought to earth the mechanical arts, technology in all its aspects, the machine.

The Greeks may have had their doubt about technology, and occasionally they worried about intellect, the impiety of the enquiring mind. Despite their mathematics and philosophy, it was felt that Socrates had gone too far: here was the secular symbol of the mythological Icarus. In Greece, where perhaps we would least expect to find it, there is evidence of the anxiety of intellectual endeavour, the concern that limits be set to man's creative imagination. It was easy enough for later peoples to magnify such concern into a baleful obscurantism, a hostility to technological and intellectual innovation that will certainly have influenced the temper of the modern age.

In historical Christianity, one of the obvious forces shaping the modern technological societies, it is easy to detect – alongside the appreciation of a 'God-given' natural world – the fear caused by the innovator, the dread of the new idea (we can find countless examples of neophobia in the historical church). Dean Rashdall, cited by Westermarck (1939), declared that one of the most deadly results of the doctrine of justification by faith is that it has encouraged the belief that honest thinking is sinful and blind credulity meritorious: 'It deters the clergy from study, from thought, and from openly teaching what they themselves really believe.' Whereas religious knowledge was thought necessary for salvation, all other forms of knowledge were sometimes seen as not only valueless but even as sinful. Paul (I Corinthians iii, 19) declares: 'The wisdom of this world is foolishness with God.' And Tertullian expressed the religious contempt for scientific knowledge in the much-quoted formula, *Credo quia impossibile* ('I believe because it is impossible'). In a similar spirit, Lactantius (in the *Divinae institutiones*) proclaimed the nothingness of all worldly knowledge; and Aquinas observed that there were circumstances in which pursuit of the truth could be a vice – for example, if we study creatures without reference 'to the due end, which is the knowledge of God'. Westermarck emphasizes the tension, throughout the Middle Ages, between the learning of the Church and the study of the classic texts, many of which had originated in pagan times and which had a scientific orientation. This has relevance to how modern attitudes to science and technology have evolved.

The Christian hostility to science has been demonstrated in countless ways over many centuries: the early opposition to the

Greek philosophers, the burning of the library at Alexandria, the murder of Hypatia, the persecution of the heretics. Galileo, old and nearly blind, was dragged before the Inquisition in chains; Darwin and Freud abused and insulted by ignorant clerics; Bertrand Russell proclaimed unfit to teach mathematical philosophy at the College of the City of New York.

Christian piety even spoke against using insights into natural law to explain such phenomena as lightning and thunder, evident 'acts of God'. For religious reasons, lightning conductors were opposed. Thus, when earthquakes occurred in Massachusetts in 1755, the Rev. Dr Price attributed them, in a published sermon, to the 'iron points invented by the sagacious Mr Franklin'. The worthy cleric noted: 'In Boston are more erected than elsewhere in New England, and Boston seems to be more dreadfully shaken. Oh, there is no getting out of the mighty hand of God!'

We do not need to give further examples in this vein. There are plenty of instances of this sort of Christian response – as well as the many wholesome religious contributions – in modern times, and they continue to reflect the familiar religious hostility to independent thought and technological innovation. This Christian response, age-old and true to the imagined primacy of supernatural worlds, must certainly have been an important factor in the shaping of the twentieth-century reaction to prodigious scientific progress and wide-ranging technological change.

The widespread superstitious dread of science and technology, evident from the time of ancient Greece to the present day, gains some support from the baleful influences of invention on human life. War was rendered a more effective pursuit by the scientist and technologist, and the emergence of the machine as a factor in the birth of the Industrial Revolution quickly stimulated new apprehensions and disquiet. It is hard to exaggerate the appalling impact of the machine on the lives of the ordinary worker in the England of the nineteenth-century. (Experiences at that time have, to some extent, influenced our attitudes to the modern machine. The early factory machines were indifferent to human welfare, i.e. *alien*. Today, for different reasons, the computerized factory system is often perceived as alien.)

Friedrich Engels, in his classic *The Condition of the Working-Class in England in 1844*, describes the pitiful condition of old and young alike. Thus, flax spinning produces a peculiar deformity of the shoulder, operatives are stunted in growth by the constant stooping and bending to low machines, and then there is the dreadful frequency of accidents and mutilation – '*The most common accident is the squeezing off of a single joint of a finger, somewhat less common the loss of the whole finger, half or a whole hand, an arm, etc. in the machinery.*'

He records that a great number of maimed people can be seen going about in Manchester. Individuals have lost an arm, a foot, part of a leg ('it is like living in the midst of an army just returned from a campaign'). Workers can be caught by straps and thrown against the ceiling above: there is 'rarely a whole bone left in the body, and death follows instantly'. Engels recorded various cases noted in the *Manchester Guardian* between 12 June and 3 August: a boy died after his hand was crushed between wheels; a youth was utterly mangled and killed by a wheel that carried him away; a young man fell under a grindstone which broke two of his ribs and lacerated him terribly; a girl died after being carried round fifty times by a strap; another girl seized by a cotton blower and killed; a bobbins turner had every rib broken when caught in a strap. In 1843, the Manchester Infirmary dealt with 962 cases of wounds and mutilations caused by machinery.

A year earlier, a report on the condition of the 'Labouring Population' noted that the accidents experienced by workers in Birmingham are 'very severe and numerous, as shown by the registers of the General Hospital'. Proper fencing was needed for machinery – 'which appears to be seldom thought of in the manufactories'. The dresses, shawls and hair of the females can be caught in the machines, as can the aprons and loose sleeves of the boys and men. Such things are *frequent causes of dreadful mutilation*. Nor are such events confined to the nineteenth century.

Already the reports are starting to accumulate concerning the impact of industrial robots in the modern world. Rolf Strehl (1955) described the strange fate of Roland Schaffer who was exhibiting an artificial man at the Chicago World Fair. The robot was said to be able to saw wood, hammer nails, and carry items from one site to another. Schaffer, at work one day, suddenly turned to see the robot advancing towards him, swinging a forging iron. The whole laboratory was wrecked and Roland Schaffer was killed. In another case, in 1946, a Milwaukee engineer was killed while adjusting a heavy robot arm that carried more than 200 thermionic valves: the mechanism collapsed, crushing the man. And in Japan, most affected by the new robot culture, there are reports of human fatalities at the hands of industrial robots. For example, the *Guardian* (9 December 1981) reported the death of Kenji Urada, a worker at the Akashi plant of Kawasaki Heavy Industries.

From the earliest times, man has been at war with the machine while his dependence on it has increased – and it is this that is at the heart of the human dilemma. There is a growing multifaceted threat from technology which, Argus-like, sees every human vulnerability. Yet the deepening man/machine symbiosis makes it increasingly unthinkable that man should abandon the machine, adopt an Erewhonian subterfuge and expel the machine makers. The machine is here in many species, propagating its kind, evolving – and now it has found a way to develop its own intelligence, a possible route to future autonomy and independence. Perceptive human observers can chart the course of machine evolution, and they can recall the early unease evinced in pagan legend and the religious tradition. It is easy to suggest that the modern threat of the machine was prefigured in the fertile imaginations of the ancient myth-makers and the fathers of Christianity. Today, man is able to exploit the power of the atom and to contrive super-intelligent machines: in so doing, he has magnified the machine threat to the point where a shadow hangs over the human race. Individual human beings have sometimes responded to the unwelcome power of the machine by enlisting in the army of machine-breakers, their activities an extreme illustration of the ebbing and flowing conflict between man and the machine.

The Machine-Breakers

Albertus Magnus (1204 – 1272) is said to have created a life-size automaton designed to work as a servant. The task took him 30 years but eventually he had contrived a robot of human appearance made out of metal, wood, glass, wax and leather. The creature was supposed to talk like a human being and to open the door for strangers. There are various tales as to what happened to the robot. In one story the automaton greeted Thomas Aquinas in the street, whereupon the worthy sage smashed it to pieces thinking it to be the work of the devil. In another tale, Aquinas waited until Albertus had died before destroying the work of many years. Another similar account concerns René Descartes (1596–1650) who is supposed to have built an automaton which he called 'ma fille Francine'. While Descartes was voyaging by sea, the inquisitive captain opened the case in which Francine was kept. The robot moved like a living being, whereupon the captain threw her overboard, thinking her to be a diabolical creation. The machine-breakers have sometimes displayed a superstitious temperament.

Later instances of machine destruction have often had a political or industrial cause. The nineteenth-century Luddites were following what Thomis (1970) has called a 'time-honoured tradition among certain occupational groups'. It is possible to trace systematic machine-breaking to Restoration times and the habit persisted well into the Victorian era. In the early phases of the Industrial Revolution, before the massive labour concentrations in the cities and the birth of effective trades unionism, industrial solidarity was difficult to achieve. The strike was rarely a useful means of bringing pressure to bear on employers, and other strategies had to be adopted – notably the patterns of machine-breaking associated with the names of Captain Swing and General Ludd. It has been suggested that machine-breaking was the basis of power in some of the first trades unions: the constant threat made local employers circumspect in pushing worker exploitation to excessive lengths. The campaigns of the Spitalfields weavers in the 1760s, for example, involved assaults on looms as a means of bringing pressure on wage-cutting employers and also on workmen who were reluctant to support the campaigns.

A London hosier who, in 1710, had infringed Charles II's Charter to the Worshipful Company of Framework-Knitters by appointing forty-nine apprentices at one time suffered in consequence the destruction of his frames. In similar fashion, frames were broken in 1779 in Nottingham; and 10 years later the *Nottingham Journal* reported the destruction of a frame of unacceptable width by men with blackened faces. And machine-breaking has featured frequently in many other industries. Thus coal-miners broke pithead machinery in Northumberland in the 1740s, and machine-breaking in 1765 won for the workers the right to choose new employers upon the expiry of their annual contracts.

It has been emphasized that the attacks on machinery did not signal any hatred of machines *per se*. Machinery was a convenient target and a symbol of the hated employer. The destruction of machines – by the London sawyers in 1768, by the weavers of 1675 opposing machines that could allegedly do the work of twenty men, by the Luddites of 1812 – represented nothing more, we are told, than the selection of suitable targets, points of employer vulnerability that could be attacked to good effect. It is suggested that the destruction of looms, waterframes, carding-engines, spinning-jennies and the rest showed no particular dislike of machines as such – but this is difficult to ascertain. It is quite possible that the Luddites and their allies saw the employers, other capitalists, and their various artefacts as a complex web of exploitation, a means of keeping the workers in penury while the employers accumulated their wealth. It is highly likely that the machines became tarred with the brush of their owners.

We incline to think that machine-breaking is less common in the modern age, though in fact it does occur – and for a variety of reasons. Pierre Dubois (1979) draws attention to how glovemakers at Grenoble in 1888 deliberately broke the needles in their sewing machines; and how, in 1895, the French railwaymen's union threatened to use sabotage to prevent the legal banning of their union. Pouget (1910) is quoted: 'With two small coins of the right shape used judiciously we can completely prevent a locomotive from running.' And Faye (1973) records how in 1970 the electrical fittings of several cranes were mischievously disconnected in the France-Dunkerque yards. In 1971 workers inserted iron bars into the lines at the Brandt works in Lyon.

On other occasions workers have deliberately run machines to destruction, operating them well beyond their defined tolerances. Taylor and Walton (1971) note how a worker let too cold a slab go into the rolls so that they were ruined. Cylinder nuts have been tightened excessively in other steelworks, sometimes causing the cylinders to crack. Is this sabotage or accident? On some occasions workers leave their machines running and expect managers to close them down. Processes may go awry, as for example happened when aluminium solidified in electrolysis tanks because of the action of Pechiney-Noguères workers in 1973. And workers have also resorted to smashing tools, factory windows, office equipment, the lodge at the factory gates, and the homes of the employers.

Taylor and Walton record how a salesman in a Knightsbridge store thrust a cream bun into a machine to stop it working, how conveyor belts are jammed with sticks, how cogs are deliberately stopped with wire and rope, how lorries are 'accidentally' backed into ditches, how textile workers maliciously cut holes in carpets, and how farmworkers choke agricultural machinery with tree branches. We do not need to speculate on the reasons for such actions. It is enough that men are attacking machines and, seemingly, have always done so. Sometimes there is a clear explanation for such action. For example, during the 1984 miners' strike in the UK there were several acts of sabotage, one of which involved the cutting of a mile-long conveyor belt at Silverdale, North Staffordshire, crippling the pit for two days. The Coal Board described this as 'an outrageous act of sabotage' that would be 'condemned by all responsible people'. The belt, weighing 20 tons, fell down the half-mile shaft after being cut. Police predictably observed that this was a 'foolish and dangerous thing to do'.

The machine-breakers have usually had industrial or political motives, though often they have been impelled to act through sheer boredom or frustration. Just as machines have damaged human health and taken human life, so men have waged a persistent war on the machine. This hostility, varying in intensity over the years, demonstrates that there is often deep resentment focused on the mechanical arts, despite the clear benefits brought to human society by industrialisation. It seems that there will always be enough antipathy to technology to sire a new generation of machine-breakers.

The Cultural Perception

There are many signs of the unease with which machines are viewed in the modern world. In comics, tales and films, robots and other mechanical devices are often portrayed as malicious and destructive, unconstrained by the finer feelings that are piously supposed to inhabit the human breast. Thus in Vaughan Bodé's (1971) comic *Junkwaffel*, aggressive machines fight endlessly on a small planet. We read, for example: 'A War of Machines Rages Across a Sterile World . . . One Goal Uppermost in the Dim Minds of the Metal and Plastic Combatants: KILL, DESTROY, ANNIHILATE until there is NOTHING left!!.' It is hardly surprising, nurtured on such material and the perennial Daleks, that children come to imagine that robots are machines of evil intent. Jasia Reichardt (1978) records some of the results of a project carried out by pupils in North West London. Five- and six-year-olds offered a number of statements about robots, including: robots kill, they strangle, they shoot people and destroy them, they keep killing and killing. Such simplistic observations may or may not be typical of attitudes in young children, but the hostility to machines that they reflect can easily be found, albeit in a more sophisticated guise, in much modern adult art and literature.

Davenport (1970) has discussed the shifting attitudes, in the artistic world, to technology in general and the machine in particular. In earlier times, he suggests, individual writers may be ambivalent, but today there is an obvious cleavage between writer and writer, artist and artist, *'with more emphasis on the negative reaction certainly'* (my italics). There is a common feeling that technology is moving too fast, that much of the stock-in-trade of the artist and writer – emotion, intuition, the creative spirit – may be swept away, and that human intelligence is now a factor threatening, rather than enhancing, the chance of survival.

Leo Marx (1964) has charted the intrusion of the machine in the works of such American writers as Whitman, Emerson, Thoreau and Melville. He notes the mixture of awe and fear with which the new technology is greeted, the aesthetic repulsion, and the striving for commercial gain. It is concluded that through the domination of the machine 'our inherited symbols of order and beauty have been divested of meaning . . . and in the end the American hero is either dead or totally alienated from society, alone and powerless'. Similarly, in Herbert Sussman's (1968) *Victorians and the Machine*, technology is seen to be transforming the landscape, stimulating artistic discussion and creating the ambivalence that is to persist in the twentieth century. On the one hand, notes Davenport, there is a joyous 'Song o' Steam' (Kipling, *McAndrew's Hymn*); and on the other is Samuel Butler's notion that machines will breed and eventually subjugate human beings. It is worth highlighting Butler's unique insights in this area.

One of the most exciting types of predictive effort is the approach that is well supported by rational thought and scientific knowledge but which is none the less prepared to make imaginative leaps. This perhaps is the essence of free thought. Samuel Butler (1835 – 1902) made a number of observations (in particular in chapters 23 – 25 of *Erewhon*, first published in 1872). In these few short chapters (a mere two-dozen pages), Butler variously anticipates the speech synthesis and speech recognition systems that are today being developed to aid man/ computer communication (*'may we not conceive, then, that a day will come when . . . the hearing will be done by the delicacy of the machine's own construction'*), that there is *'no security . . . against the ultimate development of mechanical consciousness'*, and the gradual emergence of bionic additions to the human frame. And what did Butler say about the impact of the machine?

The first clue to Butler's attitude is when the visitor to Erewhon finds himself conducted to a museum. In one of the cases there were several clocks and two or three old watches. The magistrate paused and began comparing the visitor's watch with the others – 'he turned to me and made a speech in a severe and injured tone of voice, pointing repeatedly to the watches in the case, and to my own.' When the visitor offered up his watch to have it put with the others it seemed to suit the magistrate. ('This had some effect in calming him.') Then the magistrate began to speak in a kinder tone, evidently realising that the visitor had offended him unintentionally.

Later the visitor finds out more about the museum of old machines. There was a time when mechanical knowledge was advancing at a prodigious rate, until a learned professor wrote a book proving that the machines *'were ultimately destined to supplant the race of man,* and to become instinct with a vitality as different from, and superior to, that of animals, as animal to vegetable life' (my italics). The professor carried the country with him, and the decision was taken to destroy all machinery that had not been in use for more than 271 years (a figure arrived at after a number of compromises). All further inventions were forbidden 'under pain of being considered in the eye of the law to be labouring under typhus fever, which they regard as one of the worst of all crimes'.

The civil war, waged between the *machinists* and the *anti-machinists*, had taken place 500 years before the arrival of the visitor. Half the population of Erewhon was wiped out before the victory of the anti-machinists who then treated their opponents so severely that they removed every trace of opposition. Perhaps it was remarkable that after this bloody revolution any machines at all were allowed to remain in the kingdom – but the worthy Professors of Inconsistency and Evasion argued against carrying the new principles to their logical conclusion. And perhaps it was paradoxical that during the struggle, the anti-machinists were prepared to use any mechanical device in order to secure victory. Once the war was over, all the more complicated machines were destroyed, along with all the treatises on mechanics and all the engineers' workshops – in order to cut out the evil once and for all. (This reminds us of Plato's remark in the *Georgias* about the engineer being a mere engine-maker, one whose son you would not want your daughter to marry.)

In due course the topic no longer aroused passion and was regarded as a 'curious antiquarian study'. There was a prolonged search for any machines that might have been hidden away, and new books were written to describe how the old machines worked – not with a view to reconstructing them but simply in the manner of an antiquarian describing 'Druidical monuments or flint arrowheads'.

Later in *Erewhon* some of the specific characteristics of the machines are presented, and some indication of how they came to evoke such horror. It was not, we learn, that any of the *existing* machines were feared: what caused consternation was the 'extraordinary rapidity with which they are becoming something very different to what they are at present'. Their pace of development was seen to be unprecedented – *just as today we might comment on the rate of development of computer technology.* Butler: 'Should not that movement be jealously watched, and checked while we can still check it?'

Of Butler and the other machine-conscious Victorians, Sussman (1968) observed:

> The opposition to mechanised production, the celebration of hand labour, the aesthetic distaste for the machine are but expressions of the deeper conflict between rationalism and intuitionism, between scientific and organic modes of thought that is the true subject of the Victorian writing on the machine.

It is not difficult to see this conflict echoed in many of the technological dilemmas of the twentieth century.

We often find the bald assumption that technology is necessarily hostile to many of the essential human concerns of man.

Thus Wylie Sypher (1968) assumes that 'engineering is hostile to art', recommending a return to craft practices, and concluding that 'art remains our only refuge from a technological order where all can be calculated, formulated, regulated'. This is the familiar cry that not all truth, value, worth, etc. can be computed, reduced to the formulae that can be laid up in the electronic memories of intelligent machines: there is more to life than binary arithmetic.

In common with other writers, modern poets have variously praised and condemned the inroads of technology. In the seventeenth century, John Donne was worried that science threw doubt on cherished belief; later Walt Whitman was able to remark on the beauty and power of the machine; and Thoreau was cajoled by the music of the wind in the telegraph wires. Sometimes unpromising items engage the attention of the muse. Warburg (1958) includes a poem in praise of Savery's pump, others celebrating the electric light, the threshing machine, the motor car and the aeroplane, and yet others condemning the ironworks that violate the 'muse-devoted vales' and damning the factories ('the modern rack'). In *Weep Before God* John Wain (1961) declaims:

> Next sing the machine, our glory and disgrace,
> Celebrate its possibilities and tremble
> At the cold fury of its many revenges.
>
> It began with metal.
>   Metal hates flesh,
> Hates everything that has a beating heart.
>
> Come, shape an elegy for victims of the machine!

This echoes the anti-machine sentiments that can be found in the Lake Poets and the Pre-Raphaelites (Viereck's 'aesthetic wincers').

The theatre has often responded to the encroachments of technology, sometimes in a mildly bizarre fashion. For instance, a 1924 performance (*Machine of 3000*, cast in the form of a ballet by Fortunato Depero) focuses on the love of two locomotives for a stationmaster. We find the 'locomotives' dressed in tubular costumes and required to move in a mechanical fashion. In due course, their love unrequited, they are sent off in opposite directions. Another theatrical production, *Gas* (by George Kaiser), is concerned with how technocratic organization can have a dehumanizing effect on society. Alas, the enlightened hero cannot compete with the demand for production and the workers will not heed his message.

One of the most famous fictional treatments of the technological impact is Karel Capek's RUR (*Rossum's Universal Robots*), one of several plays by the author on a utopian theme. Here a brilliant scientist named Rossum creates a family of robots designed to work for human beings. Eventually, and perhaps inevitably, the robots are used to kill people in war. In due course the robots acquire emotions and feelings and can no longer tolerate being treated as slaves by human beings. One critic saw the play as the 'most brilliant satire on our mechanical society'. Again we see the baleful consequences of new technology, a theme taken up by countless artists and writers. Davenport (1970) remarks: 'I have not been able to find any plays that are happy about the Machine world'. Nor is the situation much different in the modern novel.

E.M. Forster's *The Machine Stops* describes a society in which people live underground, totally dependent upon technology. One day the machines run to a halt, the people rush to the surface to glimpse the blue sky in a final poetic gesture, and then die because they cannot adapt to the atmosphere of the upper world. Some creatures survive, presumably to evolve and to start building further machines. Other tales portray the circumstances after a nuclear war. Thus in Walter Clark's *The Portable Phonograph* a few survivors huddle together to listen to an ancient crank-up machine: machines have destroyed their world but they rely upon a machine to preserve their sanity. And in a further comment on technological society, Burroughs has proclaimed: 'Reverse all your gimmicks . . . Reverse and dismantle your machine.' And the novelists who chose to comment in such a vein could easily find creative allies in other fields. The Surrealists like the old romantic poets, saw the machine as an enemy of nature; and there are sympathetic lines in Chaplin's film, *The Dictator*: 'We think too much and feel too little. More than machinery we need humanity.'

Films, often ambivalent or simplistic about technology, have reflected the cultural diversity that can be discerned in other artistic fields. Davenport (1970) has observed that modern and contemporary artists have feared technology *much of the time* and welcomed it *some of the time*. The film-makers also fit nicely into the generalization.

In the classic *Metropolis* (1926) the workers are slaves to the industrial complex. The machines set the pace of work, and wretched human beings toil until they drop. In an earlier film, *Homunkulus* (1916), an artificial man is only prevented from destroying the world by a sudden flash of lightning. Later films variously showed robots as endearing pets, talented servants or invincible warriors. In *Star Wars* the robots are often vulnerable and pathetic, though they are capable of violence and malicious acts. And in a host of other films, robots represent threats of one kind or another to individuals in particular and human society in general. Thus a woman is raped by a computer in *Demon Seed*; spaceship personnel are killed by computers in *Dark Star* and *2001: A Space Odyssey*; holiday-makers are slaughtered by robots in *Westworld* and *Futureworld*; and in *The Day the Earth Stood Still* the robot Gort threatens to destroy the world. And in many films – *Alien, Android, Blade Runner*, etc. – the robots are disturbingly human in appearance and manner, making their often homicidal intentions doubly horrific.

The cultural perception is ambiguous, unresolved: it reflects the complexity of technology in modern times. But there are few sanguine observers, few unreservedly optimistic prophets. There is a broad pessimism about the impact of technology, a general unease that spreads through art and literature, theatre and film. There is little in the cultural perception to allay computer fears and phobias.

The Job Stealers

The impact of technology on employment has always worried people – and with good cause. Machines have become active in one field after another, and today there are fewer and fewer jobs that cannot be performed by computer-based systems. It is a cliché of the culture that computers and robots are making workers redundant, but it is not always realized just how far this process is likely to go in the future.

In the 1970s many individual industries were drastically affected by the emergence of the silicon chip. For example, the Swiss watch industry was virtually destroyed by the manufacture of digital watches in the United States. Seventeen Swiss firms collapsed in rapid succession, resulting in massive unemployment and the loss to the US of a $200 million industry. In a similar vein, the clock industry in South-West Germany slumped because of competition from electronic timepieces, causing an employment drop from 32,000 to 18,000 in just a few years. Many of the workers in the industry are now semi-skilled machine operators, a classic instance of the de-skilling consequences of developments in microelectronics technology.

Many industries that used electromechanical components found that chips were both cheaper and more reliable. So the elimination of mechanical moving parts in cash registers led the massive firm National Cash Register to cut its manufacturing workforce from 37,000 to 18,000 between 1970 and 1975. In the same way, American Telephone and Telegraph, who supply most telephone systems in North America, reduced its production workforce from 39,200 in 1970 to 19,000 in 1976. Western Electric, a division of AT & T also estimated that a reduction of 75 per cent was feasible in the workforce needed for fault-finding, maintenance, repair and installation work. And many companies in Europe faced the same situation: the UK, for instance, saw a 30 per cent reduction in jobs in this area between 1976 and 1979. And similar trends were soon evident in supermarket chains, offices, assembly plant, design houses and elsewhere. In recent decades the textile industry has experienced immense technological innovation. Labour productivity rose more than 300 per cent over a 23-year period – and jobs fell from 581,000 in 1971 to 479,000 in 1976. There were a number of reasons for this startling employment decline. One was the declining share of world markets, and another was the powerful impact of new computer-based systems: one example is the computer-controlled jacquard knitting machine which reduces the time needed to change a pattern from the former 3 hours to a few minutes; and another innovation is the electronic mill-monitoring system which allows a single weaver to supervise a number of looms, each of which would formerly have needed its own human operator.

UK banks, introducing computers enthusiastically throughout the 1970s, saw a reduction in employment from 315,000 in 1971 to 263,000 in 1976. And we may see further reductions in staffing in the future: already there is a proliferation of automatic cash dispensers, facilities such as electronic fund transfer (EFT), and systems equipped to offer financial advice to investers and other bank customers. In a West German study carried out by Siemens it was suggested that by 1990 nearly half of all present office work could be carried out by computerized equipment, threatening millions of jobs in Europe and elsewhere.

A 1982 survey by the Economist Intelligence Unit (EIU) of 1000 jobless people found that 65 per cent blamed technology for their predicament, and a majority of those questioned thought that there was little chance of gaining employment in the near future. Such attitudes are widespread in the modern world, and there is substantial supporting evidence. All technological advances exact some price from human communities and the development of modern computers has made this process particular dramatic. It is worth remembering, for example, that the performance of IBM commercial computers has increasing a staggering 1700-fold in the last 30 years while relative costs have reduced no less than 99 per cent! It is hardly surprising that human society lacks the structural flexibility to cope with technology developing at such a frantic pace.

In many developed countries the computer is now recognized as the 'job killer' or the 'job stealer'. And it is easy to see why intelligent machines should be regarded as such a direct threat. Much human office and industrial activity focuses on tasks that can easily be formalized, allowing a computer-based system to perform as well as, often better than, human beings. The dramatic increase in the use of industrial robots is only one sign of the 'peopleless' task performance that will progressively affect one social sector after another. In Europe, for example, sales of robotic equipment was $160 millon in 1982, with an expected £500 million sales in 1985 and an annual 20 per cent growth rate thereafter. Another estimate is that UK office jobs will shrink by 25 per cent over the next two decades (cited in *Management Review*, 10 November 1983).

Suppliers of office equipment based on computers invariably point to the anticipated improvements in productivity. This means jobs. Look through the technical and trade literature and the message is always the same: seemingly the sole justification for the bulk of technological innovation is that people will be made redundant. Look, for example, at the *Application Notes* issued by Unimation Inc., the world's largest maker of industrial robots. After each individual robot application is described there is a section headed 'Justification' (i.e. details are given of why the specific application is worthwhile). Here are some *justification* extracts, taken at random:

Unimate robot feeding billets in a forging press – 'displaces one operator per shift'.

Robot processing gear blanks – 'relieves one man per shift'.

Robot assisting in die casting – 'replaces half to one worker per shift'.

Robot loading a broaching machine – 'savings of close to two men per shift'.

Robot loading refractory bricks – 'relieved the two men'.

Robot producing differential ring gears – 'significant manpower was saved'.

And so on and so forth, through dozens of robot applications. In many instances it is pointed out that the workers are saved having to perform unpleasant and hazardous tasks, which is certainly true, but the question of *alternative* employment is obviously outside the scope of the *Application Notes*. It is at least conceivable that workers may prefer hazardous employment to no employment at all, and moreover productivity increases through automation are not only being accomplished in dangerous working environments. The central justification is purely economic: if a robot, with a short pay-back period, is cheaper to employ than a human being, then it is obvious what choices an employer will make.

In these circumstances we would expect workers to resist the introduction of industrial robots and other types of automation. In 1983 it emerged that Russian workers were resisting robots (*Computer Weekly*, 11 August 1983). Even *Pravda* was compelled to observe that robots set too hard a pace and do not adapt well to such human phenomena as drunkenness and laziness on the shop-floor. The Institute for Eastern Market Research (Hamburg) suggested that 2500 Soviet robots were still in storage, owing partly to inadequate back-up and maintenance facilities and partly also, no doubt, to worker resistance. Tom Brock of the British Robot Association has suggested that this is a case of history repeating itself ('When robots were introduced initially in the US at plants such as Ford Motors, they were physically sabotaged until the workforce understood them'). Similarly in Japan, in the circumstances of a newly perceived 'computer allergy', there is growing unease about the likely consequences of increased automation. By the early-1980s, evidence was starting to accumulate about the growing resentment of computer-based systems. There were troubles with IBM and other large corporations, and many of these difficulties focused on the question of employment. For example, in late 1982 workers at the prestigious robot-making firm Fanuc were claiming that replacing workers with robots was leading their trade union to bankruptcy, as fewer contributions were received from fewer workers. The 700 members of the Fanuc union were angry that the company would not pay contributions into union funds for each of the newly installed robots, an arrangement that had been promised 2 years before when the topic of increased robotization was discussed. (Treating robots as human employees is not altogether absurd. In 1984 a special *'personal liability'* insurance for industrial robots was introduced by Skandia, the Swedish insurance company. It had been noticed that as companies became more dependent on robots, a breakdown could lead to expensive production halts. The personal liability insurance is comprehensive, providing cover for almost all the 'injuries' that a robot might suffer during its working life.) And the progressive introduction of computer-based systems in Japan has begun to seriously affect the employment of women in various ways. One consequence has been that senior workers have been shifted to simpler work in many industrial sectors, and the number of women workers has been reduced. A 1983 survey (reported in *Computing*, 24 February 1983) found that 57 per cent of companies had witnessed a decrease in the number of employees working in the computer-equipped sections, most work being given here to male workers (62 per cent of companies reported fewer female workers in these sections).

It is not surprising that such information is now starting to emerge from Japan. After all, it was here that we first heard talk of the totally unmanned factory. In the early 1980s we learnt of how Fanuc was using robots to produce robots, '24 hours a day with manning only necessary for the eight hour day shift' (Garner, 1981). And even at that time, there were hints that Japan's seemingly low unemployment rate was misleading: substantial disguised unemployment existed and would soon be aggravated by the rapid introduction of far-reaching automation facilities. It is significant that in 1980 Unimation was planning for a 35 per cent annual increase in the sale of robots to the automobile industry, one of the great international employers of human labour.

By 1984 plans were well advanced for the introduction of unmanned manufacturing plant in Britain. Already hundreds of robots had been introduced, mainly into the car industry, and as experience grew it became practical to envisage robot applications in many different fields. The Flow Systems company, for example, one of nearly two-dozen new-technology firms to have set up in the Consett industrial estate, has introduced robots to operate a night shift without human supervision. Stainless steel tubing is efficiently selected and polished by robots, without a human being in sight. Frank Turner, the manufacturing director of Rolls-Royce, has commented on this sort of manufacturing possibility. He imagines a large fabrication plant operated by only one man and a dog ('The dog is there to stop the man touching anything. And the man is there to feed the dog'). Already computers, robots and machine tools have been linked together at the Osmaston Road plant in Derby to make turbine blades for aero engines. This has resulted in a massive improvement in efficiency and productivity: in one operation, the shaping of turbine blades, there has been a productivity increase of around 200 per cent, and the employment figures are equally significant. Three men per shift can now do the work of thirty, and the anticipated increases in output are not expected to create more jobs for human beings. This circumstance has been seen as typical for economic and production trends in Britain and elsewhere: production is increasing, largely through the introduction of new computer-based facilities, and employment levels are either static or falling.

The Plessey company in Liverpool is expanding its production of components for the System X digital telephone exchanges – and, in 1984, is reducing its workforce by 825 to 2435 (though the actual job losses may be spread over 2 years). Ken Lilley, a divisional director, is conscious that the firm has been accused of slashing jobs ('in reality we are saving jobs. If we cannot achieve an appropriate staffing level for the more technological operations now being used, then the factory would simply have to close'). In British Steel a similar pattern has emerged. At Ravenscraig, for example, the time required to produce a ton of steel has been cut from 8 man-hours to 3.94 – and over the same period manpower has been reduced by no less than a half! And for the same sorts of reasons, British Leyland has cut its workforce by 20,000, at the same time increasing the number of cars produced per man from 5.98 to 14.22, by investing massively in automation. GKN has dramatically increased production, 11 per cent up on 1983 steel production at the Brymbo plant, while cutting its UK workforce by 35,000 over the last 5 years.

To an extent we are all familiar with these sorts of industrial developments. We are aware of contractions in many of the traditional industry sectors, and most of us have seen television advertisements for cars 'handbuilt by robots'. It is part of the conventional wisdom that automation is fast encroaching on one social and industrial sector after another. There are various responses to this seemingly inexorable trend. Senior managements welcome the chance to cut unit costs, to increase productivity – in effect, to lay off uneconomic human beings. Trades unions struggle to organize a rearguard action, with strikes, go-slows, technology agreements and the rest, a spectrum of devices that are largely ineffective. Unemployment continues to rise in industrial societies. Governments, necessarily, have to project a positive and encouraging image in these depressing circumstances. And so they point to the new jobs that will be found in high-technology industries, and they propose, for example, that there will be a progressive shift from old industrial employment towards new service industries. Many points can be made. In the first place, no attempt is made to broadcast the statistics of a comparison between old, outdated employment and the 'sunrise' employment of new technology. And in the second place, more importantly, no attempt is made to project how computer-based systems will be able to take over service jobs as well as the more obvious tasks in offices and factories.

One of the key elements in the new situation is the attention being given to research into artificial intelligence (AI). We do not always appreciate how competent intelligent machines will become in the near future (see chapter 7), but one consequence of this progress is that there will soon be very few tasks beyond the capacities of artificial systems. We have already see that industrial robots can be supervised by computers, and already there is talk (for example, in Jones, 1982) of how 'smart machines' will be able to dominate office work *without reference to human beings*. We know that word processors can lead to work displacement, as can the various other computer-based office systems, but what happens when truly intelligent office systems learn to communicate with each other? The human being again becomes a costly and unnecessary component in the commercial or business activity. Man is being squeezed out of one production cycle after another. This is already obvious in the industrial environment (automatic warehousing, automatic inventory control, automatic feeding of machine tools, automatic machining, automatic testing, automatic packaging, automatic cost analysis, automatic design, etc.) and in the commercial world (automatic telephone routing, automatic preparation of bills, automatic financial modelling, automatic market analysis, etc.). And how will the various service industries survive the progressive erosion of human involvement that is so obviously occurring in other social sectors?

There are already signs that computers and robots will replace human beings in service jobs. For example, robot barmen are serving up to thirty mixes of drinks in California, robot librarians are working in Japanese universities, and robot guards are on duty in some American prisons. In the library of the Japanese Kanazawa Industrial University, thirty-four 'intellibots' – small, wheeled robots – fetch and replace around 2000 video and 1000 audio tapes, on demand, for 4500 students. The robots, trundling along at a brisk 5 to 6 kilometres per hour, are able to select the tapes and insert them into players, after which they remove the tapes and re-file them. Robot guards are working, albeit in a prototype experimental capacity, in some parts of the USA. Denning Mobile Robotics of Massachusetts has agreed to supply the Southern Steel Company, the nation's largest manufacturer of detention equipment, with about 200 robots a year for 5 years, beginning in 1985 (see report in *Infoworld*, 20 February 1984). Each of the 4-feet, 200-pound mobile robots will cost around $30,000 and will be used to augment human guards: for example, to patrol prison corridors at night. Each robot guard will move at 5 miles an hour and will be able to detect human odours. One idea is that the robots could be sent on 'suicide missions' in cases of prison riot, transmitting sound and pictures for as long as they survive.

It is likely that many traditional service jobs – shop assistants, teachers, physicians, etc. – will increasingly be performed by intelligent computer-based systems. Los Angeles already has a drive-in supermarket in which an automatic 'picker' receives a computer-generated printout of the customer's order and then zooms down the warehouse corridors, under computer control, to collect the specified items. And the Tokyo Institute of Technology is developing a slender flexible robot that will be able to perform delicate surgery on human patients. Already robots are shearing sheep in Australia (see, for example, Trevelyan *et al.*, 1982; and *The Sunday Times*, 11 March 1984), and at Imperial College, London, an automatic meat-cutting system (a 'robot butcher') is being developed. Nor should it be assumed that managers are immune to the impact of computerized systems.

A recent *Computerworld* (26 March 1984) article declared that middle managers are now feeling the 'automation axe'. And this is a circumstance that is curiously problematic: middle managers are needed to implement new technology, but may find that in so doing they are destroying their own employment ('resisting or even sabotaging the implementation carries its own risk'). It is noted that over the next 10 years the implementation of computer-based systems 'will result in rapid change at all levels, from the blue-collar worker to the executive suite'. (In the same spirit, the *Guardian*, 18 December 1982, carried an article engagingly titled: 'Be kind to your bank manager, he may be an endangered species.') The perceptive manager will be less than sanguine in the present context of technological innovation.

In these circumstances it may be thought that there *are* some jobs that are sure to remain secure: namely, those in electronics and computing that are responsible for the development of modern automated system. Surprisingly, here too there are grounds for concern. Design and diagnostic engineers in electronics, for example, are finding themselves outflanked by computer systems. It is increasingly possible to feed design requirements into an automated design facility and to receive a design specification as output; and computer programs are more and more able to locate faults in electronic equipment – hence a *Computer Weekly* (3 March 1983) article headed: 'Is there a future for the service engineer?' It is often more economic to replace electronic subassemblies than to search for faulty components: and the relative cheapness of such subassemblies has been brought about largely by computer-controlled automated production methods. But surely, it may be said, programmers, systems analysts and related computer specialists will have more and more to do as we progress into a computer-dominated society. Even here there are surprising developments.

One evident trend, clearly discernible in the literature, is the progress *away from* investing resources in applications programming by highly trained human specialists. The aim is to design computers that non-expert users find it easier to access, i.e. a computer-naive person can communicate with a computer – by handwriting or by speech – and the computer itself works out how to perform the necessary tasks. What this sort of development means is that, for instance, *computers will learn to write their own programs*. In 1984 there was much talk of application program generators, software tools that would make it easier to produce programs for specific applications. Chris Naylor (writing in *Computer Talk*, 27 February 1984) asks 'Will program generators put you out of a job?', and what we find is that such devices can replace programmer activity at a certain level – but this is only the beginning! Every student of artificial intelligence knows that *Automatic Programming* is one of the main headings under which research is being conducted: increasingly computers themselves will know how to write programs. There are many pointers to this sort of innovation. Hence, Ferguson (1984) begins an article with the words: 'We, as users, understood the high-level objectives for application generators: to develop applications faster, *with less experienced personnel* and lower maintenance costs' (my italics). And in the same spirit, Romberg and Thomas (1984) discuss how a computer-based expert system can be used to produce 'more reliable software in less time *with fewer people' (my italics).*

The 'broad-brush' picture is clear. Computers and computer-based systems pose an enormous threat to human employment in the developed countries of the modern world, and few societies have the structural flexibility or the political will to cope with this developing situation. Workers, often through trade union organization, attempt to safeguard employment and income, but they have few cards to play. The old potent *'withdrawal of labour'* weapon is no longer helpful: it is precisely a withdrawal of (human) labour that the new computer-based systems are designed to achieve. In late-1983 a complaint was filed with the Federal Labour Relations Authority (FLRA) in Pittsburgh by Richard Clougherty, president of Local 644 of the American Federation of Government Employees. He charged the US Labour Department of failing to secure the employment rights of four workers who lost their jobs to a robot, but at the same time he conceded that the robot 'is probably here to stay'. One aim of the union was to force the robot 'to retire' until management/worker agreement on the case could be achieved. In early 1984 the management agreed to respect the employment rights of displaced workers, but insisted on a 6-month test period for the robot.

It is hard to imagine a future in which most productive and commercial activity is not performed by intelligent machine systems. Human beings may be tolerated in such computer-controlled configurations, but it is inevitable that they will have secondary status. Moreover, human beings may increasingly come to be regarded as an unnecessary hazard in the automated environment. There is an amusing but significant development in the Yamazaki Minokamo machine tool plant in Nagoya, Japan. Here robots have been taught to sing as they move about on the production line, to warn human workers who may stray into their path. The mobile robots carry parts from the warehouse to other robots which operate the machine tools. *And even the receptionist at this company is a robot.* It invites visitors to 'sign in', by punching their names on a console, and then the robot tells executives that the visitor has arrived.

The robot has long been perceived as a threat to people's jobs, and we have found that this is a frequent cause of computer fear and phobia. There is abundant evidence that the threat caused by computers, robots and related systems is a rational ground for human consternation.

The Omniscient Machine

The right to privacy is a central civil-liberties issue, relating as it does to the freedom of the individual in society. At one level it shows the clear conflict between the needs of the state and the needs of the citizen. Inevitably the state is keen to monitor and control, whereas the citizen wants to be left alone. 'The state's interests are served by the need to know as much about us as possible, our own by reticence about ourselves' (Madgwick and Smythe, 1974). Orwell and many other writers have advertised the dangers and horrors of the Big-Brother state. What we feel increasingly is that this issue has been thrown into sharp relief by advances in computing.

We can now store vast amounts of information on computer files, and retrieve it effortlessly for particular purposes. Moreover, networking can now link seemingly disparate computer systems, allowing a user of one system to obtain information held on another. Today, computers can 'talk' to each other, exchanging information, often across international boundaries and without public knowledge. Various studies of record-keeping in large computer-based systems were published in the early-1970s, and some of these tried to alert the public to the developing dangers. Rule (1974), for instance, saw as a principal concern the development of automated systems for mass surveillance and social control in advanced countries (see also chapter 3). Here it was recognized that large bureaucratic organizations could be enlisted to aid government activities of this sort, with formal record-keeping systems serving as a 'critical instrument'. (Rule notes in passing that credit-reporting firms are obliged to supply derogatory information about individuals to aid credit grantors in their selection of the most credit-worthy individuals.) And it is also emphasized that institutional practices may make it impossible for the public to comprehend how information about them is handled, so they are in no position to protest even if personal information is used to their detriment (the UK Data Protection Act, 1984, only goes a short way to countering this objection). One difficulty is that organizations are apt to make information available to a wide range of potential users. Hence, Rule comments: 'reports [of consumer credit reporting agencies] are available to any agency or individual who appears to be a grantor of credit. Likewise, information held . . . by the British police is . . . supplied routinely to many employers and professional bodies, as well as accidentally or unofficially to other uses.' Such possibilities are particularly significant because of the capacity of computer systems to store vast amounts of detail, some of which may be factually in error, and to convey such information to wide-ranging geographical locations in a fraction of a second. A central purpose of computer-based information systems is to speed the flow of information. It has long been recognized that this can be damaging to the privacy of citizens.

These problems exist whether information is held in a large centralized data base, or in many distributed files in a large network. There is, for example, a massive increase in the number of distributed data-processing products. A late-1970s report predicted that the value of such products shipped annually would grow at a compounded growth rate of 59 per cent; and various observers have noted the privacy and security are more difficult to control in a distributed computer environment. For example, Lobel (1982) has pointed out that much information about personnel matters will be removed from the individual's physical control, that many more people will have access to the computer, that the person obtaining sensitive information has a good chance of remaining anonymous, that information errors will spread through the system at 'electronic speed', and that, as the system expands into more and more areas, people will become increasingly dependent upon it – so the risks progressively increase. And in such circumstances there are many areas of concern to the ordinary citizen: particular threats to privacy are associated with the police, the medical services, government activities (social security, etc.), large and small companies, banks, the armed forces, etc.

It is not always realized, for example, just how extensive are the government computerized files held on private citizens. In modern Britain we now have two government departments holding no less than *113 million detailed personal records stored in 32 separate computer systems*. The Home Office and the Department of Health and Social Security now hold massive quantitites of information about British citizens, and it has been suggested that under the terms of the 1984 Data Protection Act this computerized data will become available to police, customs and tax officials investigating not only crimes that have been committed but other matters that such individuals deem to be of interest. The major computerized systems include the DHSS (with 51 million files), vehicle owners (almost 33 million files), TV licences (almost 20 million files), blood groups (11,000), landing and embarkation (1.5 million), refugee index (15,000), criminal names (almost 5 million), fingerprints (323 million), probation records (400,000), prison records (300,000), disqualified drivers (290,000), wanted or missing persons (107,000), and MI5 suspect index (18,000). The implication is that, armed only with a suspect's name, an official will be able to access these various files and to obtain the details therein. A recent case in Ipswich has been reported of where social-security officials provided the police with details of women receiving maternity benefit. A DHSS spokesman has confirmed: 'If police ask for information and a serious crime is under investigation, then information may be provided orally in confidence by a senior officer.' There are no hard and fast rules: officials are free to use discretion as to what information they reveal and to whom! (The spokesman observed: 'Clearly in life people have to make decisions – you cannot regulate for every circumstance.') It is one of the disturbing aspects of the Data Protection Bill that it legitimizes the transfer of confidential information.

The computer threat to privacy is multidimensional. Computer-based systems make it easier to collect personal information (by eavesdropping, bugging telephones, etc.), to store it and manipulate it (so linking a file on car ownership, say, with a file on political-party membership), and to hide the stored information from the citizens concerned while making it more easily available to officials. It is easy to see how effective record-keeping can exacerbate authoritarian tendencies in government and police activity – and few observers in modern Britain, for example, can doubt that the UK is becoming a more authoritarian society. People are right to feel concerned about the impact of increased computerization on civil liberties. The computer manifestly aids, in a startlingly effective way, the desire of governments and officials to monitor and control private citizens. Computers used in this way will always be represented as more efficient aids to administration, the preservation of law and order, the cost-effective provision of social services, etc. – but there is a dark side to such claims. In such socially sensitive areas, the computer represents a potential danger because it gives scope to authoritarian and repressive forces in society (see also chapter 3). There is a clear sense in which the computer can be defined as a *monitoring and controlling instrument*: this, unhappily, is also an encapsulation of the authoritarian impulse.

There is a discernible tension between human beings and machines throughout history, as revealed in mythology, religion, art and literature, and the various influences of technological innovation on social change. We see that technology has always been a two-edged force, often bringing commercial or industrial improvements on the one hand and human dislocation and despair on the other. It is impossible to evaluate the 'value significance' of new technology without considering the prevailing patterns of machine ownership, commercial dominance and political control. It is an old cliché that declares that a weapon takes on the morality of its user. The corollary is that the impact of machines illuminates the power relationships between individuals and institutions in society. When we contemplate the social impact of high-technology computers in the modern world it can be little consolation that great nations are currently governed by born-again buffoons, geriatric dogmatists and shopping-list authoritarians.

The historical tension between man and machine has invariably taken on a character appropriate to the technology and the times. It is arguable that the nineteenth-century factory equipment dehumanized human users in one way, whereas modern computers dehumanize in another. But we have seen that, whatever the contours of the conflict, there has been a continuous battle between man and the machine – with fatalities on both sides. In the past there was a sense in which the conflict could be contained: neither men nor machines could achieve the extermination of the other – if only because machine power was limited and in any case served one class of human interest. Today, however, an alarming new situation is developing, in which machines – now increasingly intelligent – are becoming equipped to challenge human hegemony in many different areas. This may dehumanize people in various ways, and may threaten human status and security. We have already hinted at how this is happening. There is more to be said.

3

The Dehumanizer

Preamble

It has long been claimed that technology has the power to *dehumanize* people in society, though this notion is not always made clear. We have already hinted at the possibilities, and it is worth again citing some findings of Davenport (1970) regarding attitudes to technology and the machine, as revealed in post-Hiroshima art and literature. The following *'essentially negative or unfriendly statements'* are relevant to the theme of dehumanization:

The machine kills the personal self, individuality, unmans man.

The machine brings material gain but spiritual, moral and imaginative loss.

The machine rhythm destroys natural body rhythm and eventually mental life.

The machine has separated man from Nature and undermined his own nature.

Technology has swept man from his moorings.

A central idea is that computers have the power to undermine human experience and enterprise, distorting the human mentality, imposing a new and inferior value structure. Scientific commentators have not been unaware of ethical and psychological elements brought by computers into the culture (some of these are indicated in the present chapter), and there are reasons for thinking that some of these influences are less than wholesome. There have been a few attempts to study the social impact of computers and their psychological ramifications. Sprandel (1982), for instance, has suggested four possible psychological effects of the widespread use of computers. He has found evidence that users can lose touch with the real world, begin to feel a loss of control, develop a compulsion for work similar to that of a gambler, and become dehumanized. These sorts of findings are echoed in the writings of other researchers (not least, in Weizenbaum, see below). Sometimes the 'dehumanization' is recognized as a distortion of interests, a rejection of social contact, an alienation from family and friends. Thus a mother typically observes of her teenage son that 'he got to look like a stranger!' – he was so engrossed in his computer. When he emerged from his bedroom, 'he was talking a foreign language! I had the idea that soon it was going to be almost impossible to communicate with him' (quoted by Kortum, *Family Computing*, preview issue, 1983). What we see here is a syndrome that has many implications and which can be explored in more detail (see chapter 5).

Some objectors claim that computers are wrongly encroaching on personal areas of people's lives, and this represents a violation of the humanist ethic. Human beings, it is argued, are an end in themselves, and excessive technological inroads can harm this special uniqueness and centrality in our vision of the world. We can only *keep computers in their place* if we maintain a clear concept of what it means to be human, if we exclude computers from areas of life in which they are inappropriate, a direct threat to the humanist concept of *Homo sapiens* in the scheme of existence. (This type of comment often has a religious flavour: how can computers begin to involve themselves in, for example, psychotherapy when they have no knowledge of the human soul?) There has been a manifest human response to the increased computerization of society. Thus Frude (1983) cites the 1965 protests at the University of California in Berkeley: a student's placard carried the words – 'I am a human being, do not fold, staple or mutilate.' Perhaps the efforts to humanize computer systems will result in people being rendered *less* human. It is easy to see the shape of this sort of development. We simplify the nature of human beings precisely in order to demonstrate how human attributes can be modelled in artificial systems: we have to *reduce* people to force them to fit within the limited parameters of computer systems. This is a clear interpretation of the process of dehumanization that characterizes the modern age. We are encouraged to view people in ways that make them amenable to monitoring, control, modelling and duplication by computer systems. We take a fraction of a person and proclaim it the whole.

The modern process of dehumanization is encouraged by a complex of forces in modern society: there are political, as well as technological, factors. But the technological factors are rapidly emerging as primary, not least because computers are gradually developing a mental competence, a spectrum of intelligence, that will eventually outstrip that of human beings. And again we can stress the simple but daunting truth that technology has the power to magnify political perfidy, bringing new strength to the arm of the despot. In the past, various human freedoms have been effectively protected by bureaucratic inefficiency. Today this type of inefficiency is reduced by computerization, while other computer-based inefficiencies render people less secure – and less human.

It can be argued that computers dehumanize people in various ways. Before exploring this disturbing circumstance in more detail it is worth examining what it means to be human. Before we can recognize threats to our *'humanness'* we need to comprehend the essence of the human being, viewed in a healthy and wholesome fashion. If the computer *dehumanizes*, in what way is it damaging our vision of man?

We can encapsulate our humanness in terms of several broad needs or features. The following are typical of these – important, but not necessarily exclusive or exhaustive.

1. We need to live in freedom, unconstrained by arbitrary state authority or repressive officialdom. We need to be able to shape our lives in important particulars – working, travelling, enjoying social intercourse as we would wish. The idea of democracy is central here, but not the *pseudo*democracy or *sham* democracy praised by politicians and others with vested interests.
2. We need to grow as individuals, nourished by new experiences and new thoughts, developing our various skills and talents.
3. We need a good self-image, a robust self-respect that is undaunted by the manifest talents and accomplishments of other people.
4. We need to be regarded by others as having independent

worth, not seen as a mere productive cog in a larger machine.
5. We need to develop ethical awareness, not in some trivial dogmatic way but so as to enhance human significance and sensitivity in the world.
6. We need to relate well to others, respecting difference, giving and stimulating reciprocal warmth and understanding. We need to be 'human-focused' rather than 'thing-focused'.

Of these six broad requirements, five are considered in the present chapter (the last is given chapter 5 to itself). What we find is that the various requirements of 'humanness' are threatened, albeit in different ways and to different extents, by the encroachment of computers in society. It is the singular hazard of computers that they represent a multilayered threat, a uniquely wide-ranging attack on human status and security. The computer partakes of the perceived odium of technology in general but has unique features of its own to contribute. For the first time in human history, technology has spawned artefacts with mental attributes.

The Dehumanizing Force

The recognition that technology can represent a dehumanizing force in society has never been more widespread: we are variously troubled by pollutants, genetic engineering, threats to civil liberties, the prospect of nuclear war, etc. We worry that animals are being hideously exploited – if not being made extinct – by technological means. We detect a creeping alienation from the world of nature, and from ourselves. In 1965 the philosopher Jacques Ellui argued (in *The Technological Society*) that we are increasingly adapting to the world of the machine but becoming separated from the world of nature. He suggested that we were adopting an alien way of thinking, concentrating on logic and problem-solving to the detriment of creativity and spontaneity. Other writers have made similar observations but from a different perspective. Ivan Illich (1975), for example, has speculated on the changed role of technology in the modern world. It used to be assumed that human action is performed within a human condition that was 'more or less given, once and for all . . .'. If the boundaries of Nature were transgressed, it took vengeance on the transgressor ('be he Icarus, Oedipus,

Prometheus or even Xerxes'). There were tools that were given to man by the gods (for example, by Hephaestus) and also illicit tools – like the wings of Icarus – that men fashioned 'to outwit the wisdom' of the cosmic nexus. Illich sees *techne*, the first mechanical arts, as a clear acknowledgement of necessity, not a route to man's chosen action. But now the old scheme has been shattered. The old limits no longer 'translate into critical thresholds for human action'. It is assumed that the old scheme provided a framework in which human beings could act with full ethical awareness: in particular, appropriate limits to the scope for human action were acknowledged, forcing a respect for the freedom of others. Now, it is argued, the human condition has been left without an ethical foundation; human action is unhinged from a normative framework. 'If this action is to remain human after the framework has been deprived of its sacred character, it needs a recognized ethical foundation within a new type of imperative' (Illich). Here it is suggested that the imperative can be summed up as: *'act so that the effect of your action is compatible with the permanence of genuine human life'*. But Illich is quick to realize that any such imperative is useless as long as 'genuine human life' is viewed as an infinitely elastic concept.

The concern here is that the startling progress of technology has shattered the old constraints on human action. Today, we *can* be Icarus and Prometheus but without the element of impiety and failure that these symbols conveyed. Modern technology has made us godlike in our powers, but how are we to estimate how these powers should be justly used? And what is the effect of such limitless power on our vision of the human condition? How is humanness to be preserved in a world that is rapidly adapting to non-human powers?

One response has been to hanker after simpler times – perhaps to the days before the Industrial Revolution – when technological innovation apparently posed fewer ethical dilemmas. Such an attitude, little more than a pious hope, is associated with the writings of the modern existentialists. They have suggested in various ways that as man is sucked into an instrumental (technological) world, he becomes a slave to it, ceasing to exist as fully personal and fully human. The philosopher Gabriel Marcel has argued that people become possessed by what they have: when human communities possess technology, there is a great (and detrimental) impact on individual human beings. In particular, there are immense dangers to our humanity as the world becomes increasingly industrialized, automated, computerized.

It is certainly easy to see the alienation at the heart of the modern world. Few people entertain real optimism about the future: through unemployment, pollution, nuclear threat, etc. many people – particularly the young – see human life as precarious and fraught with hazard. To some extent the modern existentialist talks to these people, not necessarily looking to a pre-industrial society but possibly to a post-industrial society in which the values of human dignity and individual worth are reaffirmed. It is rarely explicitly argued that this superior social mode demands the exclusion of all technology: perhaps automation and other computer-based systems will have a part to play. But it is difficult to see how the powerful dehumanizing forces, linked so intimately to the modern machine ethos, will be neutralized in tomorrow's world. Logic and experience make it easier to be a pessimist in the industrialized societies of the modern world.

Weizenbaum (1976) saw part of the problem as lying in the autonomy of the computer programmer. Other technologists – the engineer, for example – have been constrained by the realities of the material world, but the computer programmer is a *'creator of universes for which he alone is the lawgiver'* (my italics). A huge variety of imaginary universes can be created in the form of computer programs, and the created worlds act out their scripts with total obedience. We can see why such a circumstance should be so seductive to the programmer. He is master of a spectrum of worlds in which countless agents respond to his every whim. In such a realm, Weizenbaum and others have argued, the committed programmer assumes a veritable omnipotence – and again, in an entirely unexpected context, we may ask if power corrupts. The seeming omnipotence of the programmer is of course bogus. His worlds are imaginary. But they are tantalizingly able to feed his vanity, so widening the gulf between himself and other human beings, alienating him from the values of community life and civic responsibility.

In an engaging interview with John Davy (the UK *Observer Review*, 15 August 1982), Professor Joseph Weizenbaum (of the Department of Computer Science at the Massachusetts Institute of Technology) declares in all sobriety: 'I'm coming close to believing that the computer is inherently anti-human – an invention of the devil.' When he works with computers he sees himself toiling 'in the belly of the beast'. Weizenbaum's main claim to fame lies in having written the ELIZA program, a system that can hold a conversation with human beings on particular topics (most of ELIZA's fame has derived from psychotherapy sessions with a human 'patient'). Here is a typical and much-quoted piece of dialogue between DOCTOR (a subsection of ELIZA) and a young woman (whose words are in italics):

> *Men are all alike.*
> In what way?
> *They're always bugging us about something or other.*
> Can you think of a specific example?
> *Well, my boyfriend made me come here.*
> Your boyfriend made you come here?
> *He says I'm depressed much of the time.*
> I am sorry to hear you are depressed.
> *It's true. I am unhappy.*

And so on and so forth. There are now versions of ELIZA for microcomputers, and some amusing and carefully scripted conversational gambits to show the logical flaws in the ELIZA structure! ELIZA has even been hailed as *a therapeutic tool* by professional psychiatrists: one declared that the system would allow a psychotherapist to handle several hundred patients an hour, so becoming 'a much more efficient man'. It was this sort of consideration that began to disturb Weizenbaum – and the behaviour of his secretary did not help!

On one celebrated occasion she tactfully asked Weizenbaum to leave the room as she wanted a consultation with DOCTOR on a personal matter. She had been with the project from the beginning and so presumably knew the limitations of the system. Weizenbaum observed: 'What I had not realised is that extremely short exposures to a relatively simple computer program could induce powerful delusional thinking in quite normal people.' And the delusions are widespread: for example, it is untrue that computers are *'revolutionizing'* our lives – they are merely consolidating traditional power structures. Moreover, other entirely false claims are made on behalf of the new technology. It is untrue, proclaims Weizenbaum, that computers can make judgements. Whenever they have been expected to do so there have been disastrous consequences -- as in the Vietnam war. Here a mysterious 'computer sanction' was given for human war-making, even to the point when the Pentagon computers were fixed to produce false 'secret reports' for senior politicians. It is easy to see, in this, Big Brother's Ministry of Truth. *And so to delusion we add corruption.*

In an illuminating discussion between Donald Michie and Weizenbaum (broadcast on Channel 4 television, 14 March 1984), many of Weizenbaum's anxieties emerged with crystal clarity. For a start, Weizenbaum declares, the computer was born in warfare and it remains funded by the military. This alone should serve as indictment enough, but there is more. Computers are being encouraged to encroach on completely inappropriate realms. Human problems cannot be solved by computers, and there are disastrous consequences when people are encouraged to rely on them. ('I don't deny that people can be assisted by computers in some way, but . . . history will be lost . . . those things that aren't computer readable will be lost.')

The chairman Robert Hutchinson then quoted from Michie's (1984) book, *The Creative Computer*: 'The year 2500 or the year 3000 could see a planet on which humans are living in the interstices of uncomprehended incredibly intelligent electronic organisms, like fleas on the backs of dogs.'† (The theme of emerging computer life, machines as 'organisms', has its own disturbing connotation for human beings. More is said about this in chapter 5.) Weizenbaum's reaction to this quotation and to other related remarks by Michie is worth quoting in full (and verbatim):

> The deepest, best kept, very open secret which every computer person in the world knows is that most of the, specially the (sic) large computer systems that we have today are in fact incomprehensible. I say quite carefully not that they're not comprehended. I say that they're incomprehensible in principle. That's a fact. Now we've gotten ourselves into a very bad situation here. We're also increasingly urged to take human problems, and to turn them over to this incomprehensible hardware and software and so on. Have we perhaps gone in the wrong direction?

† It is worth remembering in passing that Samuel Butler, writing in 1872, depicted future man as a 'machine-tickling aphid'.

*Ought we perhaps to draw back from our dependence on machines
. . .?* (my italics)

Finally, when Michie envisages artificial-intelligence (AI) systems helping to develop 'new conceptual structures far beyond
the ability of scientists, scholars and artists, skilled people of all
kinds', and so greatly enriching and extending the 'scope of
human knowledge and life', Weizenbaum confesses himself
'appalled and almost speechless'.

In all this, Weizenbaum sees machine intelligence as essentially
alien, as a power totally unsuited to be charged with the responsibility for solving human problems. The computer is a
dehumanizing factor in the modern world because it variously
deludes, corrupts and *distorts*. It erects a false framework within
which man betrays his dignity and his worth – and the danger
is all the more pressing because the largest computer systems
are today incomprehensible to human beings, an alarming
circumstance that could hardly have been foreseen by the early
computer pioneers (the implications of this are considered in
chapter 6). Weizenbaum's anxieties are echoed by other writers,
and research into attitudes indicates that many people feel that
the computer has a dehumanizing influence. Thus, Kerber
(1983), surveying 203 undergraduates in the USA, found that
respondents regarded the computer as efficient and enjoyable,
but also as dehumanizing. This finding accorded with the
findings of other researchers (for example, Zolten and Chapanis
1982; and Mathews 1980).

Efforts to analyse what is meant by *dehumanizing*, in connection with the influence of computers, have also been made.
Shepard (1980) showed that people preferred to be treated as
persons rather than as numbers; Tolliver (1980) saw self-worth
diminishing as computers eliminate jobs; Ingber (1981) sees
human relationships distorted, as evidenced by the behaviour
of computer addicts; and Orcutt and Anderson (1977) also
detect changes in the modes of human communication following contact with computers. Such research work tends to
support the idea that computers have various detrimental
effects on human psychology: people, it would appear, are
variously rendered less social, less content with their self-
image, and less able to communicate in effective ways (there is
some suggestion that their modes of communication are 'scaled
down' to accord with what a computer, rather than a person,

might expect – for example, less sensitivity to non-verbal modes of communication). We find a spectrum of dehumanizing effects, some of them proclaimed rather than researched, but all gaining popular support in anecdotal evidence and consensual views.

There is also the broader question of the effect of *record-keeping* on human beings. Computers began, not only as super-calculators, but also as an efficient means of storing vast amounts of information. But there is a curious paradox here. Jacques Vallee (1982) has engagingly drawn our attention to the fact that the Native Americans refused to commit important information to a personal record. The white man, they believed, wrote things down in order to forget them better – not, as he maintained, to remember them more easily. And so there were the treaty violations, the breakdown of trust, and the disreputable resort to legal machinations. By contract, the giving of the word by one man to another used to be regarded as a sacred act.

This observation, which perhaps should not be taken too seriously, is taken to imply that extensive record-keeping, facilitated by the modern computer, helps to blind modern man to individual worth and ethical obligation. 'Perhaps computerised information is just another step along this road of alienation' (Vallee, 1982). We store away masses of detail, in seeming order, as if by this device we can come to terms with, comprehend, the confusions of the modern world. Technology has broken down the old safe categories, the sacred frame: we are no longer superstitious but we are no longer secure with a referential structure that gives meaning to ethics and to life. The computer creates the illusion that everything is under control, that we know where we are going. But with the same slight of hand we deepen our alienation, allow the machine to dehumanize the individuals in society. While we strive to achieve a totally quantified, *computable* definition of *Homo sapiens*, we obscure human nature in the plethora of symbols. In its capacity to alienate and dehumanize, the computer is the most potent of all machines.

Man as Component

'*It is dehumanizing to treat people as things.*' We hear this statement in feminist propaganda, in protests about appalling prison conditions, and in complaints about people being treated as numbered cogs in some vast social machine. There are many ways in which computerization can cause human beings to be regarded as things, impersonal components in some grand automated plan. Already we have seen how computer-based systems can dehumanize by forcing redundancies, a process that is bitterly resented by workers and opposed wherever possible. A recent report (*Electronics Weekly*, 25 April 1984) shows that in Eastern Europe, for example, plans to introduce robots in manufacturing industry are running into opposition on the shop floor and from the management of the factories. ('Wherever robots are imposed from above, they are usually quietly switched off.') Some automated systems are particularly unpopular. For example, the use of forge-press equipment at Voronezh, Russia, has met considerable resistance; and at engineering factories at Voroshilovgrad, Baku, Ulyanovsk and Dzhankov, 'managers merely disconnected the robots'. A key element in this opposition is the fact that too little attention is being given to human needs in an engineering environment. Workers are regarded as dispensable, high-cost components in a productive enterprise: robots and other forms of automation can often provide a more effective productive capacity – but at considerable social and psychological cost.

The increasing tendency to regard human beings as components is accelerated by the economic pressures to maximize productivity in a commercially competitive environment. Where people are not fired as redundant, or jobs allowed to disappear through 'natural wastage', then human beings have to be fitted into the production cycle. Efforts are now being made to design human beings into complex automated systems. For example, in a 1983 article (in *Behaviour and Information Technology*) Gavriel Salvendy considers the relevance of 'human aspects in planning robotic systems'. Here we find, in a highly sophisticated form, the attempt to define human beings as critical systems components in a production environment.

This sort of approach makes it necessary to ask such questions as:

1. What is the optimal allocation of functions between human supervisory control and the computer? (In other words, a human being may find himself being supervised by a computer if such an arrangement represents an 'optimal allocation' of resources.)

2. What is the relationship between the number of machines controlled by one supervisor and the overall productivity? What is the optimal number of machines that a supervisor should control?
3. What is the impact of work isolation of the supervisor in a computer-controlled environment on the quality of working life and mental health of the operator?

And then we find the chilling recommendation: *'In allocating functions between computer and humans, emphasis must be placed on optimising human arousal, job satisfaction and productivity'* (my italics). What this means in reality is that 'human arousal' and 'job satisfaction' will be estimated according to how they variously contribute to productivity. The central design objective, after all, is to produce an optimally productive system – so, for example, human job satisfaction will be defined in terms of system productivity. Inevitably, the research work is cited to justify this sort of approach: we are told that just as many people like 'simplified' work as like 'enriched' work – and so we are justified in assigning a proportion of the workers, typically those workers over 45 years of age, to tasks defined *in simplified mode*. Younger operators, we are told, should be assigned tasks that are 'sufficiently enriched to provide for psychological growth of the individual'. But what if such tasks cannot be provided in sufficient quantity to meet the needs of all the younger operators? Are they then fired, or expected to work 'in simplified mode'?

It is recognized that there are problems in arranging for human beings to work with computer-controlled robotic systems. For example, in West Germany where there was keen awareness of safety factors, a full one-third of the total robot programming time was spent on programming for safety – 'But, even in these carefully designed situations, accidents and injury to the operator do occur' (Salvendy). One consequence of this is that human beings should be assisted by computers in supervising the robot systems, but why should human beings be necessary in such a capacity? Computers are evolving as effective monitoring and control mechanisms: if human beings work with them in tandem in a supervisory capacity this can only be a temporary alliance.

There is, moreover, the question of *machine-paced work*, an increasingly common arrangement in factories and offices alike.

Here the human worker has to adjust to a production cycle that suits the parameters of machine performance. It has been suggested that more than 50 million people worldwide are today working on machine-paced tasks, and the diversity of the results obtained by research (more than 100 scientific papers) 'makes it very difficult to draw inferences which could be used to improve the working conditions on M/P [machine-paced] tasks'. Then Salvendy offers two statements which, taken together, represent a powerful indictment of the role of the machine in millions of people's lives:

> If there had not been a distinct economic advantage in utilising M/P work, there may not have been over 50 million people working in this area. It also would be true to say that if there had not been some disadvantages for the human working on M/P tasks, there may not have been over 100 publications in this area.

Some of the characteristic effects of M/P work are boredom, job dissatisfaction, and stress through undue mental load. What is particularly disturbing is that the tendency for managers to favour M/P work – because it can be nicely regulated (human beings are too disparate and unpredictable) – is influencing the patterns of human activity in many working environments. Again the machine, through a management arbiter, is itself defining the pace and character of task performance, much as it has always done in one way or another since the time of the Industrial Revolution.

It is inevitable that in a complex manufacturing environment that is being increasingly automated there will be a growing component of machine-paced work – though for fewer and fewer people. In such circumstances it is necessary to allow the surviving human supervisors enough stimulation to maintain interest and motivation but not excessive stimulation that leads to unmanageable stress due to work overload. This is one of the key considerations that influence the design of systems in which humans and robots are required to function.

The theory is that there is an optimum level of arousal, below which the human operator becomes bored and above which the stimuli become too stressful. The aim is to design jobs so that the optimum level of arousal is maintained for the human operators. Needless to say, the optimum, like perfection, will rarely if ever be achieved. In reality there will be an uncomfortable 'hunting' about the optimum, assuming that the 'arousal levels' are broadly at the right magnitude. Sometimes the operator will have too few stimuli – and so will grow bored and apathetic; and sometimes the stimuli will be excessive. In a different context, Donald Michie has commented on the latter situation. It has been found that when decision-making computer systems – in control of, say, chemical plant – become too complex, the operators tend to 'opt out'. They cannot follow the system's reasoning and so withdraw into their own psychologies. There is an inevitable danger of this sort of occurrence in any powerful computer-controlled configuration. Almost inevitably it will prove impossible to maintain 'optimum levels of arousal' for anything other than the briefest periods.

Salvendy is keen to point out that the human operator should feel in control of the plant. He should be able to override the computer if he feels that this is necessary ('the human is much more flexible to novel situations than the computer'), so there should be careful allocation of tasks between the human operator and the computer in the various stages of system design – but which operator? In which mood? And in precisely which envisaged circumstances of system evolution? The situation is highly volatile. The worthy task of trying to match human and system performance for maximum productivity is likely to prove endlessly elusive. And then what are the likely consequences for the human operators caught up in this maelstrom? It is highly improbable that they will experience optimum levels of arousal.

It is generally acknowledged by Salvendy and other researchers that human contact with robots in the industrial environment brings both benefits and problems. Productivity is increased and in some ways the safety of workers is improved. It is easier to maintain production quality and scheduling, and some new high-level jobs are created. At the same time there are problems of unemployment and de-skilling (leading to poor self-image). And in addition there are acknowledged safety and psychological problems in the human interaction with robot systems. Perhaps most importantly, underlying all the fancy research, is the stark truth that modern computer-based systems are *not* being introduced for the benefit of human operators: they are being installed in order to enable companies to survive in a difficult economic climate. Where human beings are seen to be no longer cost-effective they will be discarded, de-skilled, dehumanized. There is evidence of this process in Japan, the heartland of applied robotics.

The Sunday Times (17 April 1983) published an account of life on a Japanese assembly line, written by the journalist Satoshi Kamata. ('Instead of the callisthenics, cooperation and cosy company loyalty that we have come to expect, there is mindless toil, subservience, callousness and exploitation.') What we find here is a frightening picture, reminiscent of the darkest days of nineteenth-century industrial Britain. Workers on the Toyota assembly line were suffering every day. Kamata describes how the production line is being constantly speeded up, how a maintenance worker died, how twenty suicides took place in one year (1979) – 'While management journalism may applaud Toyota's high profit and production records, *the human costs of Toyota methods – suicides, injuries, fatal accidents, and occupational disease – increase at a horrifying rate*' (my italics).

It is likely that this industrial picture is not unique to Toyota: the same economic pressures are forcing similar practices on many international companies. Technology in general, and the computer in particular, are consolidating existing power relationships. The robot may take over completely on the car assembly lines and workers may no longer be crushed between machines, but unemployment with no adequate social security provision will not be felt by many to be a much superior mode of human existence.

Company managements are well aware that workers are apt to resist the introduction of automated systems when this leads to job losses – so schemes are sometimes introduced for retraining and reallocation (while 'natural wastage' helps to destroy the jobs of the next generation). Sometimes, management are so wary of worker reaction that they disguise the automation plans by not using emotive terms. Hence Paul Guy, director of manufacturing and engineering systems at Ford (quoted by Bruno, 1984), declared that the company had consciously avoided using the term 'robot' when it started introducing robots. Not wishing to alarm its employees, Ford chose to refer instead to 'productivity systems'. And George Poulin, vice-president of the International Association of Machinists (IAM), has acknowledged union concern, at the same time declaring that, with regard to manufacturing jobs, the worst is yet to come ('We believe that manufacturing automation's greatest impact on jobs will come during the next two to four years' – and this was said in 1984).

There is a complex of industrial and commercial pressures working to encapsulate man as a *component*. To an extent this has always been so. We know about the Industrial Revolution in the Western world, but there were consequences also for every country that struggled to industrialize. Well into the twentieth century, as we have seen, the machine has wrought havoc on human beings. In pre-revolution Shanghai, children working 12 hours a day were literally chained to small press punches: if they lost a finger they were thrown into the street to beg. It would be good to think that in the computer age the tyranny of the machine was ended. But the computer partakes of the machine essence, and has its own contribution to make to the human situation.

Skills and Self-Image

It has long been a pious hope that computers would generate new high-status jobs, and give people a psychological stake in increased automation. We have suggested that personal growth, the perfection of skills, is part of a wholesome human ethos. There would be merit in a computerized society that could aid personal growth, but the reverse seems to be happening. The computer is destroying a whole range of human activity, and de-skilling the tasks that remain. Managements have often claimed that factory automation, for example, will upgrade existing jobs but trades union leaders are increasingly sceptical. In the USA, CWA's George Kohl has commented: 'The idea that automation creates high-level jobs isn't quite true.' And he refers to a Boston College study of aerospace workers at a factory that was installing computer-based automation: only one of every five workers was trained in a high-technology area, while the remaining employees were offered low-grade service-area type jobs. ('There's going to be a disappearance of the middle-level job, and there's going to be a huge gulf between service-oriented jobs and high-tech jobs.') These observations (quoted by Bruno, 1984) are typical of worker reactions to automation in modern factories. Moreover, similar comments have been made about de-skilling in such areas as office employment and education. Thus, Tuckman

(1984) declares: 'It is equally true that, for the most part, the technological or special skill demands of existing jobs will *decrease* rather than increase' (original italics).

Typists and secretaries will be expected to use word-processing equipment but often without the opportunity to use the old skills. To a large extent, the manufacturers of word processors *intend* that existing office jobs should be de-skilled by their products. A key sales features might be that a new machine can be used 'by anyone, however small their IQ' (Parks, 1980). Salesmen often like to claim that anyone can use the new systems ('even the silliest girl in your typing pool'). The Central Electricity Generating Board reduced its number of staff at the Bristol typing centre from more than fifty to twenty-six, after introducing word processors: a supervisor was able to observe that: 'a less experienced typist is able to produce the same quality of work as a really skilled girl and about as quickly.' Word processors can perform automatic tabulation, automatic indentation, automatic right and left justification, etc.: the old laboriously acquired typing skills are no longer needed. In a recent CIS report, *The New Technology*, an observer notes that 'among the subsidiary benefits management expects to derive from [office automation] is the reduction and thus cheapening of the skills of administrative employees'.

Another sales pitch, relating to the de-skilling impact of word processors, is that the new products require less operator training. Wang, for example, has claimed that its System 30 'requires minimum operator training for maximum productivity'. Karen Nussbaum, executive director of Working Women (an American office workers association), has declared that operating word processors is dull work and can seriously reduce workers' job satisfaction. In a similar vein, Philip Kraft, a New York State University sociologist, has portrayed the introduction of word processors as 'an attempt to industrialise white-collar workers in the same way we industrialised craftsmen and artisans in the past'. He perceives the main aim as to *'replace skilled people with skilled machines tended by unskilled people'* (my italics). Kraft reckons that 'stupid workers and smart machines' are the goal for every manager in the workplace. In one view, there are already two classes of word-processor operators: the programmers, systems analysts and policy-makers ('who love the things') and the secretaries (who would 'otherwise be found in a typing pool').

Moreover, the increased specialization that is often a feature of word-processing activities can result in boring and repetitive work. This in turn generates bad morale with predictable consequences: high staff turnover, poor productivity, absenteeism, resistance to further demands, etc. And the diminished operator control over the work tends to reinforce this situation. One of the attractions of word processors is that *management* control is increased in the office environment: some machines are even equipped with logic (the 'spy in the machine') to record how many key depressions an operator makes every hour. *The New Technology* (CIS) notes that a word processor 'not only increases the productivity of the operator: it also diverts the operator of control over his or her own labour'. Wang advertising copy emphasizes the value to management of the new operator monitoring facilities ('A built-in reporting system helps you monitor your work flow. It automatically gives the author's and typist's name, the document number . . .'); and the Dictaphone Corporation declares, of its Timemaster and Mastermind systems, that they supply all the information that a good supervisor should have 'but now electronically'.

It is also clear that a number of software developments are also reducing necessary job skills in other ways. For example, there are now electronic dictionaries, making it unnecessary for secretaries to know how to spell; there are similar software packages for punctuation and grammatical formulation. Dictation equipment has already rendered stenographic skills obsolete. New technology will increasingly allow complex jobs to be performed simply by pressing buttons: fewer and fewer people will be required to operate, or to think, in a demanding or challenging fashion.

We can see how modern technology, increasingly computer based, is having a dehumanizing effect on millions of workers. Factory workers required to co-operate with robots are assigned to a new type of production line rigour; and office workers are forced to function in what has been dubbed an 'electronic sweatshop'. It is now increasingly acknowledged that many workers are coming to feel that they are effectively *controlled by their machines* (Mendelson, 1983). In such circumstances we would expect poor morale, psychological stress, recalcitrance, and increased antipathy to automated systems. Computers are de-skilling vast numbers of jobs, introducing new industrial tensions, and profoundly affecting the image that people have of their own worth, their individual significance in society.

It is well known that unemployment can lead people to think that they are worthless, fit 'only for the scrap-heap', but a deterioration in self-image is not confined to redundant factory workers or de-skilled office employees. It is significant that self-image can also be adversely affected by the development of artificial intelligence (AI) systems, artefacts that may well be charting a route to future patterns of automation. For example, in building a computer-based expert system, a *knowledge engineer* is required to extract the expertise from a human specialist: interviews are conducted until the 'engineer' has enough information to hand over to a team of programmers. The aim is to build a program that can function much as a human expert (more is said about expert systems in chapter 6). The point here is that the human expert whose knowledge is mined can find the process highly disturbing. It can seriously damage self-image to find that a life-time's expertise can be encapsulated in a high-speed computer program that weeds out inconsistencies and never forgets. Feigenbaum and McCorduck (1984) have described the experience of an expert who willingly gave his specialized knowledge over to a knowledge engineer: he 'suffered a severe blow to his ego on discovering that the expertise he'd gleaned over the years, and was very well paid and honoured for, could be expressed in a few hundred heuristics.' The first reaction was disbelief, and depression followed later. ('Eventually he departed his field, a chastened and moving figure in his bereavement.')

Artificial intelligence systems inevitably threaten our view of our own significance. Mankind, after all, has always tended to feed his vanity by contemplating his unique mental attributes. He is *physically* unremarkable: various species of animals are more beautiful, faster, longer-lived, more agile, more prolific, etc. It was always man's mind that was supposed to set him above the rest of creation: self-esteem could be made secure, it was always felt, by awareness of soul, spirit, intelligence, conscience and all the rest. Alas, machines are now evolving to be smarter than man. Scientists and scholars are now having to face what factory workers have had to contend with for decades – a machine threat to their unique, and much vaunted, competence. It is a sobering thought that just as many animals are superior to man physically, so many machines will soon come to be superior to man mentally.

The evidence is overwhelming that computers dehumanize by restricting human psychological growth, consigning human beings to a future of subservience and trivial activity. Many philosophers have urged the importance of work to human dignity, but what is meant is the importance of human growth through activity. There is no virtue in the factory or office sweatshop that guarantees long hours of toil. People need fructifying tasks that enable them to perfect their talents, develop new skills, and to escape from diminishing and stultifying labour. It is hard to see how, in the headlong rush to computerize for commercial or political purposes, this can be achieved.

The Hacker Phenomenon

One of the dehumanizing features of the computer is its capacity to distort human personality, inducing unwholesome mental states that might even need psychiatric therapy. We have already encountered various manifestations of computer phobia (chapter 2), and we have seen references to hysteria, allergy, depression and psychological disorientation induced by contact with computers. There is also the question of *compulsion*, the obsessive focus on computers to the exclusion of other worthwhile interests and activities. It is with the 'hacker', the obsessional computer programmer, that this type of compulsion is mainly associated.

It was Joseph Weizenbaum (1976) who first drew our attention to a 'mental disorder that, while actually very old, appears to have been transformed by the computer into a new genus: the compulsion to program'. He cited the programmers in the computer centres ('bright young men of disheveled appearance, often with sunken glowing eyes'). At the keyboard their attention is 'as riveted as a gambler's on the rolling dice'; they pore over printouts 'like possessed students of a cabalistic text'. Their untidy clothes, their unwashed faces, their unkempt hair testify that they are oblivious to their bodies and to the world in which they operate − 'They exist . . . only through and for the computers.' These, comments Weizenbaum, are 'computer bums, compulsive programmers . . . an international phenomenon'.

The compulsive programmer is immensely skilful, but there is a sense in which his skills are aimless. They are related to nothing apart from the machine at the centre of his life and on which they may be exercised – and his projects, without a wider frame of reference, necessarily 'have the quality of illusions, indeed, of illusions of grandeur'. His focus is such that if the hacker is prevented from working with the machine in his terms, he is apt to become depressed and apathetic, to withdraw yet further from social intercourse. He is only restored by a new opportunity to exercise his skills in the only world that concerns him. Weizenbaum has represented this condition as a psychopathology ('far less ambiguous than, say, the milder forms of schizophrenia or paranoia'). Moreover the condition is a highly developed form of a condition that afflicts much of modern society.

It is first necessary to acknowledge that the hacker is a compulsive case, and various writers (including Weizenbaum) have compared the hacker to the compulsive gambler. The compulsive gambler is concerned with the game alone: there is no focus on a careful assessment of statistics or on a prudent withdrawal when the circumstances are not propitious. Instead the compulsive gambler must persist, even when all funds are depleted and when other values – home, friends, job, etc. – are at risk. The hacker has much of the same syndrome. The only important thing is to program, to work out further technical 'fixes', to test the machine and to demonstrate personal prowess. This situation too can affect social relationships and other values that individuals might be expected to deem important. ('People get hooked. They begin to behave in a way that resembles addiction. They refuse food, they refuse their girl-friends.') Frude (1983) has drawn attention to a paper by Henry Block and Herbert Ginsburg, a piece entitled 'The Psychology of Robots'. Here we find reference to the ''computerniks'' – those starry-eyed young men who can be found loitering at computer installations at all hours of the day and night'. And Weizenbaum has instanced Dostoevsky's description (in *The Gambler*) of the atmosphere in a gambling casino:

> By eleven o'clock, there remain at the roulette table only those desperate players, for whom there exists only the roulette table . . . who know nothing of what is going on around them and take no interest in any matters outside

the roulette saloon, but only play and play from morning till night, and would gladly play all round the clock if it were permitted.

Such a description, it is suggested, might equally apply to a typical computer room.

The compulsion of the hacker has been described in various terms. He is variously said to be addicted to the computer, fixated on the machine, obsessionally pre-occupied, subject to illusions, etc. Often he treats the computer as if it were a person, reprimanding it, cajoling, recriminating . . . sometimes he is even said to be in love with the machine (see chapter 4). In all this there is an unwholesome distortion of mental life. Other interests are sacrificed, and there is progressive withdrawal from contact with other human beings – unless they happen to be hackers. Thus the compulsive programmer exists in an unreal world inhabited by personified computers and other addicts. It is part of the danger of the computer that it is able to seduce people in such a fashion. And the hacker pays a price for his compulsive commitment: withdraw him from the computer and he becomes disoriented; allow him to continue with his obsession, on his terms, and he is likely to experience *'burn-out'*.

The addictive character of the hacker condition is well described in personal confessions that sometimes surface in the computer literature. Thus Lenore Weiss (1984) describes how he was reduced to addiction by contact with the computer: 'I was getting my jollies mainlining on the terminal. I had become a computer junkie and didn't know when to quit.' It is suggested that perhaps the computer documentation should enclose a Surgeon General's warning – *Only to be set up near a window where you can preferably see at least one tree*. In such a way, the compulsive terminal user might be able to seek distraction when the seductive power of the computer threatens to become overwhelming.

Weiss talks about 'wildly' thumbing through a manual, feeling 'sweat rolling down the back of my neck', 'feeling the old burn-out syndrome pulsating down to my hands'. Here there are symptoms akin to those experienced by computer phobics. The computer both fascinates and terrifies. The addict can spend time with other pursuits, in the hope that the compulsion will diminish, but the ploy is likely to be only temporarily effective. So Weiss works the soil, despite the rain –

'until my next computer fix' (my italics).

The computer junkie is today often described in computer journals. Thus Nancy Welles, writing in *Datamation* (15 June 1984), notes the hackers' compulsive use of computers ('there's something addictive in the power of the hardware or software'); and an MIS executive who has worked with hackers is quoted. It is suggested that days spent at the computer is their kind of bender, a consequence being that they can have difficulty 'talking and dealing with other people'. Carl Reynolds, vice president of communications and data processing at Hughes Aircraft in Los Angeles reckons that computer junkies are just a fact of life. He comments that 'some percentage of the population is in A.A., some is on drugs, and some is going to end up banging on computers all the time'.

Compulsion, addiction, delusional thinking . . . the computer stimulates them all. A manager comments on the typical employed computer junkie: 'They don't want to do the job they've been hired to do. They'd rather stay in fantasy-land, where they know everything that's happening.' And with the fantasies of omnipotence, experienced by the hacker in his unreal world, we even encounter megalomania. There is increasing concern that the distortions wrought by the computer on highly capable minds are symptomatic of a broader condition in modern technological society. Perhaps we are betraying human nature by trying to capture its essence in an inappropriate symbolic scheme. The hacker's distorted view of reality – and his disordered priorities – are simply a more extreme form of a confusion that afflicts all modern computerized societies.

The Repressive Computer

The computer is increasing its involvement in politics, to the growing alarm of many observers. Much of the computer activity in this area is concerned with processing statistical information and other data relevant to the administration of a modern state. Computers can also model financial circumstances and the likely impact of certain policies on issues of the day. Already, in this fashion, computers are being encouraged to adopt a judgemental role. We can already see how AI systems could be developed to provide advice, on an interactive basis, on a wide range of political matters. If computers are not yet politicians, they are well on the way to becoming top-ranking civil servants!

It is inevitable that computers used in a political advisory role should come to acquire Big Brother associations; and indeed, long before that stage is reached, politicians are still nervous about broadcasting their excessive reliance on computer-based systems. Thus in the 1984 US campaign for the Democratic nomination, local campaigners made efforts to play down the role of technology in their efforts. *Computer Weekly* (8 March 1984) reported that 'activists also worry about public perceptions of the latest vote delivery mechanisms, and dread the Big Brother label that is often attached to their methods'. And the anxiety is not restricted to what we may choose to regard as the computer-naive public. Joel Bradshaw, a campaign consultant to Gary Hart, has observed that *'political people are intimidated by computers'* (my italics), a circumstance which, if true, is a disturbing reflection on the competence of politicians to administer highly computerized modern societies. But this generalized unease is only one aspect of the Big Brother syndrome. There are other considerations that are even more alarming. For example, there is the extent to which computers serve to consolidate highly repressive regimes in Latin America and elsewhere. It is far beyond the scope of this book to chart in detail the prevalence of human rights violations in Brazil, Argentina, South Africa, etc., but there is no doubt that such violations are aided rather than discouraged by the availability of high technology, including computers.

Assassinations, kidnappings and torture are a commonplace feature of many dictatorships and oligarchies throughout the world, and computers serve to aid the activities of repressive forces in such countries. Penny Lernoux (1982), for example, in an extraordinary exposé of repressive events in South America, has indicated the importance of computers in helping governments to collect and exchange information on political refugees. Nadel and Wiener (1977), writing for the computer industry journal *Computer Decisions*, have pointed out that US companies have sold sophisticated computer systems to Chile, Uruguay, Argentina and Brazil to identify political suspects for interrogation, torture and execution. It was reported that the Argentine Federal Police were using high-technology electronics for repressive purposes: for example, use is made of the complex

Digicom system for controlling civil disturbances. The board of directors of E-Systems, a supplier of military and police electronics to Argentina and other (then) totally undemocratic regimes, includes Admiral William Rayburn, a CIA official during the Johnson administration.

Computer Decisions also highlighted a 1973 document disclosing IBM plans to sell a 370/145 computer and forty 3270 terminals to the security department of Rio de Janeiro, Brazil. It is said that the deal did not go through at the time, perhaps because IBM realized that among the normal Brazilian police projects was 'J41, Political Activists'. But IBM did in fact sell 370/145 computers to Chile – to Chilean universities controlled by the military. The National Council of Churches tried to stop IBM selling computers to the Pinochet regime (the director of the Council declared: 'When you know who Hitler is, you can't pretend you don't know what he's doing with your equipment'). And Senator Edward Kennedy noted that the Ford administration had denied him information on whether US computer companies had been selling computers to foreign police agencies unless he would promise to keep the information confidential. It was also stated by Juanita Kreps, once President Carter's Secretary of Commerce, that it would be against the national welfare to provide information on the export of US computers to foreign police and intelligence agencies. Yet there can be little doubt that such sales consolidate the power of repressive regimes.

Computers were also enlisted to sanitize activities in another repressive regime, namely El Salvador in 1984. A computer and other equipment were set up by the Central Election Council to create the impression that the totally fraudulent national election had some democratic significance, i.e. that the electoral register was adequately compiled and that the voting procedure was well conducted. In fact chaos reigned and the official charged with computer responsibilities later dissociated himself from the whole dismal process. Here it had been assumed that the presence of a computer and other electronic equipment would project a modern high-tech image, suggesting that Salvadorean democratic processes deserved respect. In the event, the opposite impression was generated: the computer was exposed as an absurd toy in a political morass.

In 1982, *Computer Weekly* (7 October) published a remarkable article, entitled *'How the trade in computers helps to crush human rights'*, showing how the mandatory arms embargo against South Africa – passed by the United Nations Security Council in November 1977 – has been constantly violated by Western states. And this 'to the delight of computer manufacturers' (Rout and Lawrence, 1982). Today computer manufacturers flout the 1977 embargo (and also the 1964 embargo) with the tacit encouragement of Western governments. In 1978, a year after the USA had signed the UN embargo, IBM sales to South Africa increased by 250 per cent over the previous year; and today President Reagan is giving active support to South Africa's ambitious militarization programme. Similarly, in 1978, the British computer manufacturer ICL – under a Labour administration – won a contract to supply a South African police computer. Today ICL machines are used to run the notorious pass system: details are stored about hundreds of thousands of black workers who face imprisonment if they are found without their pass-books in the white areas of the country. ICL has refused to give details of such orders but has maintained that it will trade with any country where such activity is legal under UK law. An Amnesty International report revealed the further use of technology for repressive purposes: the managing director of ICL-South Africa is quoted: 'Our computers are quite extensively used by the Bantu Boards in administrative jobs. We also have a computer which stores information about the skills of blacks.' The Bantu Boards are also using computers supplied by Burroughs, NCR and Mohawk Data Sciences. Linda Rout and Bridgette Lawrence, in the *CW* piece, also mention reports of goods from ITT, Westinghouse, Digital Equipment and Plessey being used for repressive purposes in South Africa.

Moreover, computers do not need to be used for specifically repressive purposes to have bad effects on the mass of the populaton in authoritarian regimes. A massive poverty study of South Africa, financed by the Carnegie Corporation of New York, has revealed that one-third of all its black children under the age of 14 years are stunted in their growth because they do not get enough to eat; there is one doctor to every 174,000 blacks, who have an infant mortality rate 31 times higher than the white rate. And while the blacks starve, the whites export food to make money. An ominous finding of the 1984 Carnegie enquiry is that many of the migrant jobs, the sole source of income for millions of blacks, are now drying up – because of the spread of high technology, including computers. One consequence is that *1.43 million blacks have no income at all*, compared with 250,000 in 1960. In South Africa the computer and other fruits of Western technology are working to further stratify an already appallingly stratified society. Black unemployment is increasing, nutritional diseases are becoming endemic, and Western companies supply the computers to help the security forces keep the lid on the explosive situation.

Nor should it be thought that computers only serve repressive impulses in such obviously authoritarian regimes as Brazil, El Salvador and South Africa. In March 1982, details emerged in the UK about a secret MI5 computer capable of holding intelligence files on millions of people. Connor (1982) noted that the existence of this system posed 'grave questions about parliamentary democracy as well as personal data protection and privacy'. It has been obvious for many years that both MI5 (concerned with internal national security) and MI6 (external security) were working to expand the scope and number of their individual records. As far back as 1974 it was declared that there could be no assurance that such records were 'either relevant or accurate' (Madgwick and Smythe, 1974), and that their main purpose appeared to be to 'keep tabs on politically suspect persons'. Today we know, for example, that records are kept by MI5 on 15 000 Communist Party members.

It should be obvious that the secret accumulation of masses of personal information – where the individual has no means of checking its accuracy – is highly relevant to the question of civil liberties and human rights. (The 1984 Data Protection Act is irrelevant since its provisions do not apply to various excluded data bases.) The March 1982 revelations stimulated much debate – most of it fruitless. Parliament had at no time been informed of MI5 plans to acquire computers with 20,000 million bytes of on-line store. We may take it as significant that the ICL dual 2980s which comprise the system were acquired in secret. 'No record of the 2980s exist on the confidential ICL files on the location of 2980 series computers in the UK' (Connor); and many observers have speculated on why MI5 needs such massive on-line storage capacity (twenty gigabytes, in the jargon). The Ministry of Defence has only been prepared to comment that the computers are used 'in the intelligence field'. But bearing in mind that MI5 is concerned with *internal* matters, it is precisely this intelligence connection that concerns people.

Apart from the machinations of governments with a natural interest in monitoring and control, there are many potentials for abuse in the computerized recording of personal information. We have already indicated the size and scope of computer data bases dealing with personal information in the UK (chapter 2), and it has been estimated that by the end of the 1980s, about one-fifth of London's entire population will be on computers operated by Scotland Yard. Michael Meacher, Labour MP, has commented – along with many other observers – that computerized data bases 'are vulnerable to espionage, eavesdropping and error'. Pounder and Anderson (1982) have drawn attention to documented cases of abuse, involving the Police National Computer (PNC), by ex-police officers. In one case (*New Statesman*, 23 October 1981) ex officers of the Thames Valley police force allowed vehicles to be checked, using the PNC, as part of a private investigation. And Chief Inspector P.A. Fraser of Merseyside Police has highlighted (in *The Behavioural Implications of Computers*, Home Office Library) other instances of computer abuse, showing also how such abuse can be covered up. In one case, a local-authority computer operator in West Germany accepted money to erase criminal convictions from the police computer system. The culprit was merely dismissed from his employment 'to avoid the embarrassment to the police that would have been caused by a court case'.

Many other cases of this sort could be cited. In 1981 it was found that members of the public could infiltrate the Police National Computer -- so procedures were changed; in the same year a Thames Valley police officer was suspended following allegations that details of cars and criminal records had been leaked from police computers; in 1982 the then Home Secretary William Whitelaw was asked to investigate claims that the Police National Computer was being used to vet hotel and catering staff in London; and in 1983 and 1984 there were further suggestions and allegations that data held on police and security computers was open to abuse. Lawrence (1984) describes the increased use of computers by North Yorkshire police, commenting: 'While there is no suggestion that North Yorkshire is abusing the facilities . . . to the detriment of civil liberties, it is easy to see how a change in the political climate could bring this about.' It was further claimed, in a dossier drawn up by Mr Julian Jacotter, a Labour member of the Thames Valley police authority, that information from police computers could be illicitly sold for between £4 and £15 a check, though the Thames Valley police claimed that access to the computers was restricted to a small number of police officers.

A number of complaints have been made that computerized files held by Special Branch are not totally secure (1982 saw more than 1 million Special Branch files transferred into a computer). In January 1982, in the UK, *The Observer* newspaper reported that it had obtained details of a Special Branch file on a law-abiding member of the Social Democratic Party (more than 10 years before, this person had helped to arrange anti-apartheid demonstrations, but he has no criminal record). At one time Special Branch files on anti-apartheid activists were compiled as standard police procedures in various parts of the UK. After *The Observer* had informed Scotland Yard of the information it had received about the SDP member, the Special Branch suspended telephone enquiries, changed the number of its computer bureau, and ordered all enquiries to be made by teleprinter.

There have been cases in the past where Special Branch files have been obtained by employers. One such instance was revealed in 1980 when the police apologized after an erroneous Special Branch file cost a woman a job with Taylor Woodrow, the construction firm. This highlights the need for adequate control over how the police collect and store information. Progressive computerization of police files gives greater rather than less cause of anxiety in this context.

For example, there are grounds for concern in the working of the computer-aided Berufsverbot, the West German method of vetting public-sector employees. According to an article in the prestigious journal *Computing* (28 June 1984), there have been more than 5000 public-sector dismissals over the past 10 years – on the grounds that such people represented security risks. The people discharged from employment have included railway drivers, postmen, university lecturers, teachers, pig-breeding experts, cooks, swimming-bath attendants and at least one part-time gardener. Since the Second World War, West Germany had conducted no less than 3 million investigations into personal loyalty to the constitution. This prodigious activity has involved massive information-gathering that would not have been possible without the computer.

Today West Germany is implementing massive computerization as a means to citizen surveillance. For example, Nadis, the computer of the German Secret Service, is only one system amongst many in a highly integrated network, with all major police computers connected to the central police computer (Inpol) via a two-way link. Moreover, the police have automatic access to the files of local government. What do we make of the remarkable fact that the West Germans have amassed details of 4 million terrorist suspects (almost one in eleven of the whole population)? The Interior Minister of Bavaria has commented, 'there are thousands you have to observe'; and border police have been instructed to note those persons carrying one of 287 publications or belonging to one of 239 organizations. This degree of surveillance would be totally impractical without the singular contribution of the modern computer. Those who doubt that Big Brother is already amongst us need look no further than Berufsverbot.

The repressive computer is not the product of some fevered imagination. It is already in place and working on a day-to-day basis in many countries of the world. And even in countries where there is supposed to be a secure history of civil liberties the computer is evolving a threatening potential for repressive action. It is easy to say that the computer is merely a tool, taking on the attitudes of its users, but there is more to be said. The computer actively encourages a view of man which feeds the repressive impulse. The computer expects man to be numbered, quantified, monitored and controlled. In this circumstance the computer holds immense authoritarian promise for the future. This conclusion may be seen to be doubly threatening when we realize that the computer has, for more than a decade, been interesting itself in political campaigning.

The Campaigning Computer

We have seen that there are many ways in which computers are encroaching on 'human-significant' areas. Perhaps one of the most worrying examples of this sort is how the computer is being enlisted to 'program' political candidates. Throughout the 1960s and 1970s, immense strides were made in simulating – by means of computers – a wide range of economic, psychological, military and business situations. The idea was that if you could run a computer simulation for a particular scenario, your subsequent decisions in that situation would be relevant and informed.

Richard Wirthlin – who was to become involved with Ronald Reagan's political ambitions – founded his company Decision Making Information (DMI) in 1969, by which time he had gained immense experience in simulating economic and business situations. He was also skilled at obtaining information about the US population from the thirty-eight Federal Government statistical agencies from Census to Education. (His work – in particular, his involvement with Reagan – is well profiled by Roland Perry (1984) in his startling book, *The Programming of the President.*)

In 1970, Wirthlin developed a computer simulation to aid the re-election of Reagan as Governor of California. By developing a computerized approach to polling, Wirthlin could use the system to measure public attitudes to the candidates, whereupon Reagan could tailor his campaign accordingly. (Perry: 'The model continually tested how well the packaged Reagan themes were being accepted by the public and compared this to acceptance of the themes of Unruh's campaign.') And the experience gained by Wirthlin in the 1960s and 1970s was used to help Ronald Reagan to the White House in 1980. Wirthlin and his team had directed Reagan's every move by reference to an array of sophisticated computers. When Reagan was elected, Wirthlin was given a new task. Thus, according to the blurb on the Perry book – Wirthlin was asked 'to develop a computer system that would guide the Presidency in much the same way he had directed Reagan to win the 1980 election. *The computer had come to power.* Politics and government would never be the same again' (my italics).

The use being made by Ronald Reagan of computers to judge public opinion and responses has caused one report (in the UK, *The Sunday Times*, 29 April 1984) to ask: 'Is 1984 the year of the computer-programmed candidate?' Already we learn that DMI is being paid $1 million a year to program the president, using the most sophisticated computer system ever developed for use by a campaigning politician. The idea is that this system (Political Information System, PINS) will guide the president's actions and words until election day. Needless to say, this gives immense power to Richard Wirthlin. ('While Reagan may not change his beliefs to suit a computer, his style is certainly programmed to fit the strategy dictated by Wirthlin's polls.')

And so here we are – the day is fast approaching when the computer will tell the American president what to do and what to say, when he will not trust his judgement unless it is confirmed by symbols on a screen or on computer printout. This must be one of the ultimate hazards – that we must believe such and such because a *computer* says it is so. This was one of the criminally damaging effects of using computers in the Vietnam war: such effects could all too easily be writ large in a nuclear confrontation.

The Ethical Perception

The authoritarian significance of the computer assumes that it is possible to progressively desensitize people to ethical considerations. There should be no doubt on this score. No national populace is so morally sublime that we can be sanguine about the security of civil liberties. There is too much historical precedent to have illusions on the matter: people are easily corrupted by the political fashion of the moment, and by the technological demands made by every new toy in the hands of policy-makers. It is also disturbing that computers have a peculiar influence on ethical sensitivity, as if they are a new breed of intelligent creatures propagating a new value system.

John Sutherland, in a recent *Guardian* article (12 April 1984), has drawn attention to how human beings respond to a display on a word-processor screen. If we catch someone in the office reading a letter we incline to avert our eyes, but the words on a word-processor screen attract our attention, beckon us forward. The influence of the ubiquitous television receiver is manifest: we have already been conditioned to believe that anything that appears on a display screen is effectively published, i.e. made public. But this is a disturbing situation when we are constantly being exhorted to abandon paper in favour of electronic communication (everyone in computing knows that the 'paperless office' has been a buzz-phrase for years). One of the most heavily promoted features of the electronic ('paperless') office is the electronic mailbox. Messages are left in a specially allocated mailbox file in the computer, in the absense of the intended recipient; when he returns he accesses the file and displays the day's (week's) messages – but with what degree of privacy. Of course, he could view the display in his own office; the problem can be overcome. But what is interesting is that a strange amorality descends upon the office staff in connection with screen-displayed data. They may be told that such data was private, but would they believe it and would it affect their actions? Sutherland draws an analogy with those old people trained to purchase in small corner shops, who cannot resist shoplifting in supermarkets. ('They don't see helping yourselves as theft.') It is suggested that most computer-owners 'steal without a qualm – because they don't see it as stealing'. For example, people may acquire copyright-protected software on a computer course, and photocopied manuals (again copyright-protected) may be distributed in the same fashion.

The implication is that high-technology computers can somehow neutralize ethical awareness, encourage people to act in a fashion that is unrelated to the proprieties of the situation. Audiences are encouraged to identify with the boy in the film *War Games*, who uses a modem to break into the school's computerized records and change his examination grades. It is the way he does it. 'What *War Games* insinuates is that being able to handle a computer with virtuosity puts one above common morality' (Sutherland). And what is true of the young computer buff next door has a wider significance: the high-tech specialists behind the American onslaught on Vietnam displayed an almost insane amorality – such people, doubtless good fathers and responsible citizens, were prepared to countenance with equanimity the computer-aided slaughter of millions (the full story of the computer impact on the Vietnam War has yet to be told). And if consciences can so easily be anaesthetized in a 'local' war that involves merely 50,000 dead Americans and 2 or 3 million dead Asiastics, can we be complacent about the computer-based preparations that are being made for the ultimate nuclear conflagration?

The point is that high technology, particular computers, is not ethically neutral, but affects profoundly the ethical perception. Perhaps this is due, at least in part, to what Weizenbaum saw as the delusions of grandeur to be found in certain types of computer professionals. Perhaps it is due also to other causal factors not yet identified and understood. But the multifaceted response to the hacker phenomenon, as one aspect of the current computer scene, shows at least a certain ethical confusion.

The amoral computer enthusiast (as in *War Games*) invites audience sympathy and identification, and this is no mere fiction. The skilled hackers working on the West Coast of America in 1983, who illicitly cracked military and civil data banks, were variously written up as 'whizzkids', 'superbrains', etc. They even made the front page of *Newsweek*. And when we find an article headed, 'The FBI goes after hackers' (as in *Infoworld*, 26 March 1984), we do not automatically assume that the hackers are disreputable social elements to be brought to justice at all costs. At the same time there has been much time and effort spent on making hacking a crime. Peggy Watt (1984) describes the attitudes of California lawmakers to proposed anti-hacker legislation, and at around the same time *Computerworld* (16 April 1984) records that New York Attorney-General 'expects the Empire State to become the 21st state in the union to make hacking a crime when a bipartisan bill is passed later this legislative session'. In announcing the bipartisan approach, it was observed that the computer *'has created a whole new area of crime'* (my italics).

This situation has many ethical implications. In the first place it is clear that the computer has extended both the scope of crime and the methods for combatting it. Then there is the public response to computer crime, of which hacker activity is only one manifestation (computer crime is often sanitized by the image of the computer as a high-tech modern marvel). And underlying such considerations are the changing ethical attitudes of actual computer users, whether hackers, office workers, government officials, etc. There are ethical factors in the computer revolution that have scarcely been addressed.

Another aspect of the developing computer scene also deserves mention. It is characteristic of computer systems that they discourage human-to-human contact, and it should be remembered that it is precisely in the contact between people that ethical sensitivity develops and matures. Computers work to destroy the very social framework in which human beings grow to ethical adulthood. Consider the following:

1. Teleconferencing, a principal element in the electronic office, makes is unnecessary for people to meet in order to hold a face-to-face discussion.
2. Electronic mail, again a much-vaunted pillar of the office-of-the-future, discourages telephone calls. 'Mr A may not be there. Better to leave a message in his computer file.'
3. Home terminals have the result of discouraging employees

from commuting to the office. Instead they work in a domestic isolation. A data entry clerk, who needed socialisation, commented: 'I got so tired of staying at home I started talking to myself' (quoted in *Infoworld*, 23 April 1984).
4. Factory 'communities' are increasingly likely to comprise computers, robots and a small (and reducing) number of human beings.

What we are seeing in the progressive computerization of society is the gradual destruction of human-to-human contact, the elimination of traditional social intercourse, the projection of a new model for human life – in which individuals work and play in contact with computer terminals rather than people. We see this trend in the addiction of the young to computer games; the growing support by massive vested interest for the electronic office in which people talk to people (if at all), not by speaking in the same room or on a telephone, but via the ubiquitous keyboard; the growing reliance among specialists, in whatever discipline, upon computer-based expert systems, rather than upon their peers and colleagues; and the removal of increasing number of workers from the social climate of the industrial complex – to the relative isolation, usually in impoverished circumstances, of home or institution. We are seeing the computer working to destroy whole areas of human social intercourse, and to progressively impoverish the human social contact that remains.

This is a situaton with profound and disquieting ethical implications. If only a part of this scenario is accurate then it reveals one of the most far reaching trends to dehumanization of *homo sapiens* ever accomplished by new technology. And the ethical impact of the computer is not only felt in the damaged social fabric of the factory or office complex. It is found in the hospital, the school and in the home. People are being encouraged, in whatever walk of life, to turn away from people and towards machines. This unrelenting pressure is being felt in the most intimate relations between human beings (see chapter 4). The computer is mounting a colossal threat to man's ethical sensitivity, and in this daunting circumstance we see the most wide-ranging influence for dehumanization. For it is through ethics that all human life is mediated: the ethically insensitive society is indifferent to social deprivation, cruelty and the prospect of war. The progressive computerization of society encourages the amoral atmosphere in which the ethical perception is dulled, confused, impoverished.

What we find is that there is a multilayered threat to our humanness. Technology in general and computers in particular encourage the viewing of people as components in mechanized systems: it is not simply that human needs are assessed in order to design convivial automated equipment – what is happening is that a limited set of parameters is being used to define the human being. Designers of word-processor terminals, for example, are interested in the effects of screen glare on eyesight, of chair rake on back fatigue, etc. This design focus takes into account a narrow subset of the many factors that are relevant to the physical and psychological health of the human being. But the approach is seductive: it suggests a scientific interest in human welfare, whereas in reality it constrains people within a narrow framework of productive activity. 'Human-factors engineering' will be quite unable to adopt a humanist reference until it broadens its philosophy, looking to an ethical concept of man that transcends the mundane daily hours spent hitting a keyboard.

We have also found that computers are diminishing human skills and adversely affecting self-image, effects that go deeper than merely wounding self-indulgent vanities. There is a threat to human purpose and human dignity – and to human health. The hacker syndrome shows how computers, like the gambling saloon, can stimulate a compulsive fixation, distorting the psychological perspective, disordering natural priorities, and working to the detriment of human relations. This has relevance to the ethical perception, the spectrum of insights and experiences that enable people to grow as individuals in human society. The computer is not ethically neutral: it has unique features that encourage an amoral perspective. The hacker who succeeds in cracking military and commercial systems, in itself manifestly illicit activity, is openly applauded as a computer whizzkid. He may or may not be making a protest about the tawdry machinations of the military-industrial complex or about the socially indifferent money-grubbing of the multinational corporations: we cannot deduce the hacker's politics, if such exist, from the character of his computer pursuits. The central point is that the hacker's technical brilliance anaesthetizes his conscience – and the ethical response of a public who would be ready enough to lynch a juvenile delinquent caught carrying a jemmy, or a Communist Party member picking up military secrets. The computer stimulates amorality, at the same time – through its all-pervasive 'monitoring and control' capability – consolidating and developing the repressive impulses of the political state.

The computer's dehumanizing role, evident in many ways and at many social and personal levels, is likely to stimulate a range of fears and phobias in those people who perceive it. There are many other dehumanizing forces within society. The computer has worked to strengthen their arm – and to add further baleful influences of its own.

4

The Alternative
Love-Object

Preamble

Human relationships face many threats – unemployment, poverty, physical or mental illness, adulterous affairs, etc. – and we now see how computers can be added to the list. At the simplest level, computers represent a seductive focus of interest, an alternative commitment that can pull devotees away from friends, lovers, spouse. To some extent any deep interest can have the same effect: thus we hear of 'golf widows', 'photography widows', etc. But with computers there is a much more insidious element, since computers – alone among artefacts – have started to acquire humanlike attributes.

We are accustomed to viewing inanimate objects in anthropomorphic terms. The old family car may be dubbed 'Ethel' or 'Jemima' to signal the affectionate regard normally reserved for human beings and other animals. But we do not really believe that a vehicle can be personalized to the point where it may be said to be an actual person, e.g. having a personality and the power to respond to situations in an intelligent fashion. If we say that a particular camera 'doesn't like hot weather' or an old typewriter 'has a will of its own', we know we are talking metaphorically. But what is exciting and alarming about computers is that such concepts as analogy, metaphor and mimicry are giving way to literal truth! It is one of the disturbing aspects of intelligent artefacts that they are beginning to acquire personal qualities. And in such circumstances the threat posed to human relationships by computers is sometimes akin to the threat posed by other human beings.

This chapter indicates some of the ways in which computers are currently undermining human relationships, and how this trend is likely to continue in the future. In the role of an 'alternative love-object', the computer works to disorientate human affections, to bring disorder to the spectrum of priorities that help to define our humanness. We have already seen how computers can represent a dehumanizing force in society (chapter 3). In their impact on human relationships, they show in yet another way how the dehumanizing process is developing.

The Fictional Frame

The idea of human beings developing relationships (sexual and other) with computers and robots is a familiar one in fiction. (Sometimes the plot hinges on a bizarre antifeminism, as in the film *The Stepford Wives*.) Often the basic idea is that only through *artificial* creatures will men and women find the truly idea companion or lover. Thus in *L'Eve Future*, by Villiers de l'Isle Adam, a book first published in 1891, the hero falls in love with a singer and comedienne who, though physically beautiful, has a common and silly personality. An electrician friend of the hero offers to make an exact physical replica of the singer, but without her mental shortcomings. The upshot is that the hero learns to love the artificial creature, only to lose her when the ship in which they are travelling is consumed by fire. He declares: 'I shall not grieve except for this shadow.' In another tale, Lester del Rey's *Helen O'Loy* (first published in 1938), it is the robot's turn to mourn. The beautiful android Helen is sent by her manufacturers to work as a housekeeper for two bachelors. In due course she falls in love with one of the men, marries him, and destroys herself when he dies, so that she may be buried with him.

In a strange story by Maria Bujanska, *Krwawa Mary* (Bloody Mary), published in Warsaw in 1975, a young woman is abandoned by her lover in an unusual skyscraper called the Hotel Fotoplastikon. She is detained here for months, served food by automata who say nothing apart from announcing the time of the next meal. Eventually the desperate woman rings an alarm bell, whereupon a male robot arrives and introduces himself as a PUBLIC LOVEROBOT OF THE PASSIVE TYPE – WITH THE COMPLIMENTS OF THE MANAGEMENT WHO WISH YOU A PLEASANT ORGASM – DETAILED EXPLANATION IN THE CUPBOARD. All this fellow is prepared to say is 'coitus interruptus is bad for health – I only serve for the purposes of internal discharge'. Only after this creature, a number of other robots and her returning human lover are destroyed is the woman able to escape.

Sometimes fictional machines are not as satisfying as the real thing. In *The Cyberiad* by Stanislaw Lem (1972), the great designer-inventor Trurl is charged with the responsibility of saving Prince Pantagoon from the pangs of love. To achieve this difficult task he makes 'an erotifying device stochastic, elastic and orgiastic and with plenty of feedback'. Whoever is placed inside this device experiences 'all the charms, lures, wiles, winks and witchery of all the fairer sex in the Universe at once'. The idea was that the Prince, so stimulated, would forget his lost love. Alas, the machine fails: the young man emerges from it pale and weak and with the name of his beloved on his lips.

Some modern fiction develops the idea that computer replicas or simulations of human beings may well be indistinguishable from flesh-and-blood creatures. We will see that this is an increasingly common idea in discussions of the relationships between people and artefacts. If the artificial devices do differ from human beings this only serves to illustrate their superiority as friends and lovers. In fiction, human beings are already at a disadvantage when trying to compete for affection with artefacts, and there are signs that this fictional dream is being slowly translated into reality.

In Christopher Hodder-Williams's *Fistful of Digits*, the hero Peter is in love with Christina. She finds herself taken over by the computers and quickly develops a split personality: one moment she is herself, the next a committed spokesperson for the computers that control her. Then the computers hit upon the notion of creating a simulation of Christina, to confuse Peter further. He finishes up thinking that he is talking to the real Christina via a television screen, where in fact he is only com-municating with a fabrication. The computers are wily enough to use the real woman as the programmer, since she alone is intimately acquainted with Peter's emotional responses. The real Christina eventually dies, but the computerized embodi-ment of her lives on.

What we see here is a celebration of the theme that human beings can react to intelligent machines much as they can react to other people. It is this possibility that represents the under-lying threat to normal human relationships. There are many ways in the modern world in which this growing threat is manifested.

User-Friendly, Computer-Friendly

Today everyone in computing, and a good few outside it, know that 'user-friendly' is one of the fashionable buzz-words. It has had currency for several years, but it is only in the 1980s that *user friendly* has been so freely spread around to denote types of keyboards, software, screens, dialogue formats, display conventions, microcomputers, etc. The idea is that people should be able to interact *effortlessly* with intelligent machines. The design of keys to press, screens to view, software-controlled behaviour to observe (and respond to), etc. should not be such as to effectively *discourage* the human user. More and more computer systems are interactive, i.e. they can encourage human comment, responding appropriately with observations, advice, etc. The human being may even key in 'HELP', whereupon the computer will display the information or guidance that the human user requires. The aim is to make interaction with computers trouble-free, easy-to-manage, without stress or tension, i.e. to make it 'user friendly'.

The current emphasis on user-friendliness has largely been stimulated by commercial pressures. Buyers of computers will necessarily gravitate to systems that do not appear threatening or unduly complex. The more *friendly* a computer, the more human beings there will be who enjoy sharing its company. Many of the input innovations – the mobile 'mouse', the touch-sensitive screens, the emerging capacity for voice understanding, etc. – have been researched and developed solely to maximize the user friendliness of modern commercial computer systems. There are grounds for thinking that *true* user friendliness is a mirage, an elusion – computers are necessarily alien in their intelligence and in their modes of working – but the search goes on for mechanisms that will aid human/machine interaction (this is, for example, a central impulse in fifth-generation research).

The term 'user friendly' was first used in the 1970s: for example, Kogon *et al.* (1977) identified a 'growing trend to user-friendly systems', and countless writers have used the term since that time. Stevens (1983) notes that 'user friendly' can have a quite literal meaning but that 'in general the term is *a metaphor of a seductive but restricting kind'* (my italics). *User friendly* is necessarily a term that disturbs people since it encourages the notion that a specifically human attribute – friendliness – can be attributed to machines. If the attribute *can* be so attributed, then there are the most profound implications for man/machine relations; and if the attribute is necessarily totally unsuitable as an adjective for any computers that are, or ever might be, then hundreds of thousands of people in the modern world are strongly wedded to a delusional mode of thinking.

We have already seen that people working constantly with computers may develop simplified communication habits, modes of verbal communication well suited to computers but poorly suited to intercourse with other human beings. The mirage of true 'user friendliness' can only exaggerate this tendency. Again a restricted definition of friendliness is influencing prevailing attitudes to communication in general: people are being encouraged to see effective communication as facility with automated systems. The massive weight of advertising copy is not representing user friendliness as a desirable long-term feature in computer systems, but as an actual prevailing characteristic in available commercial products. Yet the term, misleading to purchasers and users alike, is not even helpful, as presently conceived, to the systems designers themselves: 'the concept of user-friendliness as at present defined . . . is neither meaningful nor helpful to the systems designer' (Stevens, 1983).

What is happening is not that computers are being designed to emulate human modes of showing friendliness, in any full sense, but that human beings are being encouraged to adapt to the restricted communication abilities of modern artificial systems. What this means in practice is that people should ignore all the manifest subtleties of human/human communication, and adapt to intelligent artefacts that are much less capable. There is thus a two-fold dehumanizing process at work. On the one hand there is commercial pressure for people to turn away from other people and to focus on communication with machines; and on the other there is parallel pressure for people to restrict their own communication scope in order to accept a concept of 'friendliness' as exhibited by the narrow capabilities of modern computer systems.

Moreover, there are many criticisms of current user-friendly designs to the effect that they do not even achieve their limited aims. Thus a banking terminal that repeatedly displays the message 'HOW CAN I HELP YOU?' becomes irritating with constant use, a point that is also made in connection with the MICKIE interviewing system. And the error messages in some so-called user friendly systems have been criticized as unnecessarily abrupt and incomprehensible to many users. This implies that true user friendliness, a worthy aim for some purposes, has yet to be achieved in any meaningful sense – even within the terms of an extremely parochial definition of 'friendliness'.

The reverse side of the user friendly coin is that human beings appear to have a natural impulse to personify all manner of things. This tendency, discussed as animism by Neil Frude (1983), led to early religion (where trees and rivers could be assigned personalities) and to many strands in art and literature over the centuries. Piaget found that children up to the age of six tended to regard all things as conscious ('Why don't stones die like insects when you put them in a box?', 'Does it hurt food when you eat it?'). As children mature they tend to direct their animistic impulse at other types of objects, and the same inclination survives, albeit in a transmuted form, in most adults. They are thus psychologically disposed to invest machines with human attributes, even though there may be scant good reason for such an activity.

The upshot is that not only are computers being given a (pseudo) user friendliness but human beings are already disposed – at one level – to be *computer friendly*. This is the paradox: that computers, for many reasons, stimulate a host of fears and phobias; and at the same time beckon people forward to enter into friendly relationships (or, as we have seen, the extremes of compulsive fixation). This paradox necessarily creates a certain tension in the human/computer connection, and adds to the confusion in our image of intelligent artefacts.

It is worth summarizing the central points made in this section:

1. There is immense commercial pressure for a computer user friendliness that in reality is bogus.
2. People are being encouraged to adapt to the narrow communication potential of modern computer systems, i.e. to

impoverish   their   natural   human   communication competence.

3. People, through the age-old animistic impulse, respond well to pressures that encourage the anthropomorphic interpretation of intelligent machines, even where this diminishes our human nature.

4. The tension, between computer-generated anxieties and our willingness to personify artefacts, deepens the confusion in how we regard modern computer systems.

These various pressures and tendencies are likely to develop and intensify in the years to come. They will be linked in various ways with the growing insistence that computers and robots be regarded not merely as *entities with personalities* but as *living systems* (see below). This circumstance will further seduce people into turning away from human beings and towards machines, and will deepen the process of dehumanization that is already so clearly discernible in modern society. We will see that computers and robots will not only come to serve as our main industrial and commercial colleagues but also as prime objects of affection: as companions, friends, lovers.

Computers as People

Jasia Reichardt (1978), with many other observers, has remarked that the closer a robot resembles a human being the more familiarity it can engender. The same is true, *mutatis mutandis*, of the computer: where the robot may manifest physical similarities, by dint of possessing torso, limbs, etc., the computer may exhibit mental similarities, by dint of mathematical or games abilities and also, on occasions, by virtue of unpredictable responses. Thus the then 9-year-old James Fischelis can declare at the Hertfordshire Dolphin Camp, a scientific centre: 'A computer is a bit like another person. You can play with it and work out problems with it.' In 1980 the researchers Karl Scheibe and Margaret Erwin suggested that it might be a mistake to regard the computer as a neutral agent, and explored the tendency for people to react to the computer as if it were another person. Twenty male and twenty female undergraduates were asked to play computer games, with the degree of computer intelligence allowed to vary from one game to another. Some of the games were played in a room with only one terminal, the subject and the experimenter being the only people present; other games were played in a room with twelve other terminals, most of which were being used. All the comments of the subjects, while they were playing against the computers, were recorded on a tape recorder.

It was found that only one of the players did not speak at all. The others made an average of thirty-four comments each. The sex of the person made no difference, but subjects seemed more inclined to talk when they were in an isolated position. The subjects made a total of 358 pronoun references, variously referring to the computer as 'it', 'he', 'you', 'they' (and even 'Fred') – never as 'she'. There were various types of comments – remarks, commentary, questions, exclamations, etc. – and profanity was often employed. Scheibe and Erwin make various suggestions in the light of this research. For example, it is proposed that the compulsive programmer is a totally new personality type created by the interactive features of the computer. They present examples of people who get angry with computers, sometimes accusing them of deliberate mischief or dealing with them in affectionate language. Above all, they conclude that the computer can easily be cast in the role of another person. *Time* magazine even managed to declare a computer its Man of the Year for 1982 – to the alarm of *Computing* (13 January 1983): '*Time* has done us all a disservice by choosing a computer to grace its cover . . . By focusing on the machine, as *Time* has done, we just confuse the issue.'

The personification of computers is revealed, above all, in the language used to denote them. We have noted the use of personal pronouns, as revealed in the Scheibe/Erwin research. Metaphor can also be employed to signal an effective anthropomorphization of intelligent machines. The use of the word *intelligent* (and its various synonyms – *smart, bright,* etc.) is the classic case in point. For many years, intelligent was always put in quotes when denoting certain types of peripherals, terminals, computer systems, etc. – as if to indicate that the user did not really mean to imply that the artificial system had mental attributes: an 'intelligent' terminal was still only a bag of tricks. But then the situation changed: the ubiquitous quotation marks disappeared and computer people became increasingly willing to recognize that certain types of machines could be regarded as truly intelligent. And what is true of *intelligent* will also come to be true of other mental metaphors. In due course, computers will be variously said to *know, perceive, think, feel, choose, create,* etc. What starts off as metaphor and analogy evolves into accurate literal description, and the 'person credentials' of intelligent machines become ever more robust as computers become more sophisticated.

Frude (1983) has noted 'the fact that there seems to be a fundamental willingness to accept the machine as almost human'. This leads to a host of questions, not least the character of the man/machine relationship that is likely to emerge. There will be pressure – again from commercial sources – to develop computer systems to which human beings will feel attracted and which in consequence they will wish to acquire. Computer-based systems will be given appealing voices and sympathetic dispositions: they will enquire after the user's health and make appropriate remarks at carefully judged intervals; they will offer compliments and advice – at all times working to refine their mannerisms and conversation through the feedback acquired in a fully interactive situation. In such circumstances, true user friendliness will have been achieved – but at what cost to human-to-human relationships. After all, a computer would presumably not have moods – or could switch them on and off to achieve particular personality effects – and would never lose patience (unless as a deliberately calculated ploy to stimulate the human companion). The computer friend would make relationship mistakes, but would constantly learn from them and would never forget! It is easy to see, in such circumstances, how human beings could come to prefer intelligent machines to other people. There are plenty of signs that this is already happening.

In Love with Machines

Affection for computers and computer-based systems sometimes takes some curious forms. A case was reported (the UK *Guardian*, 24 October 1981) of a worker who had programmed 'his engineering skills, both mental and physical' into a numerically controlled flame-cutting machine. When he operated the machine it was like watching his own brain at work. Finally, when the machine was sent away after 8 years for modernization and repair, the grieving man sat at home for 10 months without pay rather than be transferred to another machine. The worker is described as a 'man who fell in love with his machine'. The provocative question asked in a woman's magazine – 'COULD YOU LEARN TO LOVE A ROBOT?' – has already been answered.

A mini cab driver has told the UK *Guardian* reporter Jane McLoughlin (1 November 1983) of his remarkable affair with a computer. He quite literally loved the one he used, caring for it, feeling jealous if anyone else wanted to use it: 'I used to stay on in the office to use it . . . I'd ask it things like 'Do you love me', and because I'd programmed it, it always gave me the right answer. Although I knew what it would say, the fact that it printed it out by itself *made me believe there was really a relationship between us*' (my italics). Alas, technology moved on and the man was forced to break the relationship with the out-of-date machine, but 'almost with the exaggerated reaction of a rebound from a broken love affair, he now loathes everything to do with computers'. In this case, the man outgrew his addiction, helped by the rapid pace of technological change. Others are less fortunate, and there are inevitable consequences for marriages and other intimate relationships.

Deborah Wise, writing in *Infoworld* (14 February 1983), declares, with tongue in cheek: 'The age-old love-story formula has been rewritten for the eighties. It reads: Boy meets girl; boy gets computer; girl loses boy; boy gets girl a computer; boy loses girl. The moral: computers win.' We are invited to consider a new record single ('BASIC ain't the language of love', sung by Steve and Debbie Brown and available from Reymont Associates). In this song-for-our-times, Harry and Charlene have a happy, loving relationship until Harry becomes besotted with hardware and software (Charlene laments: 'One day a personal computer took my Harry from me', to a snappy little country melody). Charlene decided to compete with the seductive power of the micro – 'One night I thought I'd give it one extra shot. I wore a plunging neckline and showed all that I'd got' – but to no avail. All that Harry is prepared to do is to buy Charlene her own micro, which – the tables turned – she comes to prefer to Harry (the machine 'asks for nothing in return'). But are they both happy?

We may take this song – which, incidentally, is largely based on an actual case – as a light-hearted parable on the modern age. It is an accurate enough comment on our modern priorities, and on the disturbingly seductive power of the intelligent artefact.

Marriages under threat

In the Australian feature film *Crosstalk* starring a supercomputer, the I500, there is the following piece of dialogue between a man and his mistress where the man tries to justify to his mistress his machine fixation:

He: Cindy, I thought you understood, appreciated what I'm trying to do here.

She: I did, Ed, I did . . . past tense. It's just been too bloody long. You have lived and breathed those machines of yours to the detriment of everything else, including me. Even when we make love I feel like I've just got your body. Your head's off screwing the I500.

Not for the only time a fictional film suggests the possibility of a sexual relationship between a human and a machine.

There is accumulating evidence to suggest that excessive commitment to computers can be immensely damaging to marital and other close relationships, much in the way that a third human being (forming one element in the 'eternal triangle') can represent a hazard. For example, where employees are given home terminals relationships can suffer. A case in point is the successful Electronic Information Exchange System (EIES), set up by Professor Murray Turoff in New Jersey. A study of how this nationwide system is being used has been made by sociologist Roxanne Hiltz, and there have been alarming findings. Users became increasingly dependent upon the home terminals ('I can't think when the computer is down'), and wives would complain at other times (a frequent remark was 'You don't talk to me now – you're always on that damned computer'). And at least two divorces have been attributed to prolonged contact with EIES.

The mini-cab driver reported by Jane McLoughlin had marital problems because of his intense relationship with the computer. In fact his wife thought that the man was having an affair with a woman, and repeatedly asked him to explain why he stayed until midnight at the office when everyone else went home at 6 o'clock. At one stage she asked him to move out, changed the locks, and told him not to bother her and their two sons. In another reported case, a husband had an affair with his secretary *because she was a constant reminder, in bed and at breakfast, of the computer at work.* His wife, the effective antithesis to that environment, never knew about the secretary; instead, she thought he spent all his spare hours at the computer. Another case concerns Daphne who is married to a computer man who, despite loving her and their son very much, prefers to live in his own computer world. He began working late, and Daphne suspected another woman. Later she realized that he was simply obsessed with the computer: 'I couldn't compete – not with a machine, for God's sake.' And Daphne compares the event with a middle-aged man having an affair with his young secretary ('I'm afraid that if he's phased out by the firm for younger people, losing that computer may break his heart').

The specialist computer press is not unaware that enthusiasm for computers may be detrimental to marriage and other relationships. Michael Rossman (1983), for example, writes in *Creative Computing* 'Of Marriage in the Computer Age'. Here we find Mary and Kevin having marital problems because, after making love, Kevin would get up and start work on the computer. 'As the computer revolution invades ordinary lives, couples find themselves tangled in domestic conflicts involving the machine and its effects' (Rossman). In another case, a wife is jealous of her husband's contact with an Apple microcomputer 'as if it were another woman'; in one couple, the wife becomes obsessed with the computer and starts trying to program her husband by writing him lists. Some psychiatrists have noted that the computer can deepen existing conflicts within a marriage with unusual and remarkable force. Therapist Marcia Perlstein, quoted by Rossman, has observed: 'Computer involvement tends to be compellingly hypnotic, as addictive as a drug. It can be *worse than another lover* as a competing force for attention – totally involving, always available, and quite demanding (my italics).' And the threat persists even when the afflicted person is no longer at the terminal. The problem is still occupying the mind: the computer is really never left behind. ('Even for a mate who is not jealous and who appreciates his passion for the keyboard, it can be quite a strain.') Moreover, the computer *invites* involvement, *encourages* addicts to neglect other problems – which may be problems in the marriage – and to retreat into the comfortable, but illusory, realm of the imagination. It is easy to retreat into the computer to avoid domestic pressure. And it is men, rather than women, who are more likely to be afflicted (women are the ones who 'stand by baffled as their mates disappear in abstract obsession').

Various therapists have suggested that men are apt to use their enthusiasm for computers to escape from the problems of relationships. Serious computer activity can stimulate the impulse to spend time on abstraction, at the same time discouraging the expression of emotion in a personal human-to-human relationship. Some men are already inclined to withdraw when they feel the pressure of difficulties in a relationship: the computer encourages this withdrawal – so making the problems worse. Dr Michael Evans, a Berkeley psychologist, has suggested that computer programmers 'tend to be a fairly neurotic bunch anyway, made more so by the character of the machines and tasks they work with . . . programmers tend to be introverted people, high achievers, prone to anxiety, and, of course, quite obsessive . . . All this affects their abilities to begin and to maintain relationships.' Only rarely can they talk in any detail about their work to their wives or girl-friends, and even when working they tend not to relate effectively to other people, being pre-occupied with the abstract technicalities of the job in hand. Programmers are encouraged to relate to computers rather than to people, a circumstance that is increasingly affecting the domestic environment with the spread of home computers. 'All this is tough on relationships' (Evans).

Married couples are increasingly caught up in the computer vortex. There is constant massive propaganda to encourage every family to acquire a home computer – and not simply in order to play games, which can be addictive enough, but to learn to program, to explore with increasing skill the *hidden mind of the computer*. It is suggested that the problems posed by the computer for the modern marriage are real and massive – 'and often intractable' (Rossman, 1983), because the difficulties are demanding, complex, demanding of time and consciousness, and a constant strain. We are expanding our vision and knowledge through increased access to intelligent machines, but at a growing cost to traditional human relationships.

Jean Hollands, recognized as one of the leading US experts on 'silicon stress', has observed that there are more marital problems in the data processing industry than in any other walk of life, and she regards herself as providing therapy to women who are constantly having to compete with computer systems for their husbands' attention and affections. A 1984 report from Cognos Associates of California underlined the marital difficulties at the heart of the American computer industry. This report, entitled *Changing Lifestyles in Silicon Valley*, showed that Santa Clara County had more divorces, 10,900, in 1980 than the number of marriages. A cross-section of women living and working in Silicon Valley were interviewed, most of whom have moved into the area: about a half of the women were divorced.

It is increasingly recognized that success in the data-processing world often leads to undue stress, divorce, alcoholism, drug-abuse and 'burn-out' (which we have already met). Some guidance is available to couples who face these sorts of problems. For example, Jean Hollands' best-selling *The Silicon Syndrome: A Survival Handbook for Couples* gives advice to couples facing the stress and other problems brought about by the rapid expansion of the computer industry. The typical Silicon Valley couple is where the husband is the scientist/engineer, and the wife has little or no technical background. In the few cases where the woman is the high-tech type, the same observations can be made, but with the labels switched.

The pattern is always the same – computer technology starts to encroach on the marriage, the computer is preferred to the spouse, and inevitably the rejected partner begins to hate computers and all that they stand for. Helen Appleby, a Silicon Valley worker, told *Computing* (15 March 1984): 'It's not too bad if you're single. It's the married couples, especially those with kids, who start to become unstuck.' It is recognized that one of the most important impacts of the conflicting loyalties between computers and other commitments is the effect on interpersonal relationships – marriage and the family. A spokesman at the Santa Clara Sheriff's Office was reported as saying that the problems relating to alcoholism, drugs and child-abuse were reckoned to be higher than the national average. Even Gary Cline, marketing manager for the Gaba company, is forced to admit that 'this is an involving type of industry . . . I admit that a lot of people in computing jobs do not see enough of their families'.

What we see is a multifaceted picture in which computers and computer-related technology are damaging human relationships in many different ways. At the heart of this situation is the extent to which computers can represent an alternative focus of interest, absorbing time and effort, making an overwhelming and seemingly irresistible claim on human commitment. At present, computer-based systems, already seductive enough, are imperfect surrogates with clear physical limitations. Even the most fanatical devotee would find it difficult to enter into a truly intimate *physical* relationship with today's computers and computer-controlled artefacts. However, this situation is likely to change in the future.

The Robot Lover

We have already seen that the robot lover is a familiar enough character in literature. Modern films (e.g. *Demon Seed*, *Westworld*, etc.) are also well acquainted with the idea, but can it be entertained as a practical possibility? Will intelligent artefacts come to be alternative love-objects in the most literal sense? There are plenty of people who think so.

Al Goldstein is an American magazine publisher, tending to focus on such colourful titles as *Gadget, Cigar, Death* and *Screw*. The English journal *New Scientist* (27 October 1983) notes that according to an issue of *Technology Illustrated*, which devoted several pages to Goldstein and his interests, the man is fascinated by robots. He is quoted as saying: 'My fantasy is to . . . phase the wife out of the picture, to come home and hear a robot greet me . . . My wife knows she's on the way out. She's like a buffalo. She knows she's here temporarily until technology catches up.' And the same thought has struck certain women who exploit male sexual predelictions in order to make a living. According to W. J. Weatherby, writing in *The Guardian* (23 February 1983), there is an alarming 'red-light recession' in New York, where the prostitutes apparently share some of the fears of other workers – that technology will put them out of a job. There is now a thriving trade in sexual aids of various types: dolls to fondle and have sex with, vibrators, artificial vaginas and penises. One female prostitute in New York complained: 'It won't be long before customers can buy a robot from the drug-store and they won't need us at all.' And before the feminists rush to put pen to paper, we should point out that some women entertain fantasies about acquiring male robot lovers. Edna O'Brien, sad that 'love and its appendage sex is a single ticket on the Via Dolorsa' (*The Observer*, 13 February

1983), has decided that there is only one thing for it – 'to move with the times and go technical'. If Steven Spielberg can fashion her a Love Object (LO) 'that is tall, greying, handsome, intellectual, humorous, moody (just for a little spiciness) and incurably besotted by all 120 lb of me', then she will happily say goodbye to 'Tolstoy, face masks, rendezvous and those sweet anonymous insinuations that wend their way on the feast of St Valentine'. She may not be pleased to learn that a computerized robot has now been made of Andy Warhol, at the cost of some $400,000. Warhol once declared that he 'wanted to be a machine', but now his friends are worried that they will not be able to tell which is which.

We should not underestimate the scope of artificial sex aids, once the appropriate companies learn that there is money to be made by linking such devices to computers and suitable sensors. Already the dolls sold for sexual purposes to lonely men can be highly complex instruments, though not yet computerized. Some come equipped with washable vaginas so that the necessary hygienic precautions can be taken; and expensive models may have small electric motors to cause the vagina to vibrate whilst in use; or caressing fluids may be exuded from the mock-vaginal walls. And it has long been possible to buy mock sexual organs for either sex, a concept which is as old as mankind but which has only recently benefited from the ministrations of high technology! One device can be inserted over the human penis, whereupon the artefact gives out warm moisture from an internal spongy sleeve and uses a quiet electric motor to provide an 'incredible pumping action'. The advertisement for this device (a 'technological breakthrough in erotic bliss') carries the alarming question – *'Could it really be better than the real thing?'* Again the feminists should note that there is a plethora of mock penises, and here actual therapeutic progress may contribute to the technological possibilities in the field of commercial sex aids. In late 1983 it was reported (*The Observer*, 2 October 1983) that a hydraulically operated penile prosthesis had been successfully developed.

This device is surgically implanted and designed to bypass impotence by allowing an erection at any time. A prominent psychiatrist Dr Paul Weisberg has called the device 'one of the craftiest examples of American ingenuity in this century'. Already it is estimated that the implant has been made available to more than 15,000 American men, a figure that is reckoned to represent only a fraction of the total market. Another expert Dr Gary Alter, a Los Angeles urologist who performs about sixty penile implants a year, has suggested that impotence affects between 5 and 10 million men in the USA (one in ten of the male population).

The device itself is a clever piece of engineering. After an incision is made under the penis, two plastic cylinders are inserted and fastened to a sac, located in the lower abdomen, containing saline fluid. A miniature pump secured in the scrotum is used to push the fluid into the penis, a procedure that allows an erection to be maintained almost indefinitely. A release button on the side of the pump is used to return the fluid to the abdominal sac. Dr Scott, who has performed no less that 1300 implants at St Luke's Hospital in Houston, claims a 95 per cent success rate. Patients are said to be immensely enthusiastic: a retired civil servant reckoned that it saved his marriage, a Californian physics professor declares that the operation stopped him from committing suicide, and an author regained the self-confidence needed to complete a novel.

The point about this seeming digression is that the artificial penile prosthesis is highly relevant to the emergence of computer-controlled robot lovers, a disturbing possibility that will come to fruition when – doubtless for commercial reasons – a number of disparate industries combine to generate a new class of intelligent artefacts. Once the sex-aids industry and the robotics industry realise that there is commercial scope in mutually beneficial co-operative activity, then the robot lover will become a functioning member of society – with what consequences for traditional human relations we can only begin to imagine.

Already we can see how such a robot system may be contrived. As one simple illustration we do not need to go beyond the artificial vagina. Such an artefact could be controlled by a microprocessor linked to various sensor devices. The sensors would detect the motion and hardness of the penis and feed appropriate signals to the microprocessor. The micro in turn would cause the vagina to respond accordingly, varying its gripping action (by means of rubber or plastic 'muscles') and its moisture emissions (from miniscule apertures linked to a micro-controlled pump) so as to maximize male pleasure. And we can speculate in the same fashion, *mutatis mutandis*, about the male robot lovers that may be acquired by women. Here sensors in the artificial penis would quickly detect the state of a vagina. The penile hydraulics could cause the penis size to vary to aid the vaginismus condition, and to gently exude suitable fluids in circumstances where vaginal lubrication was insufficient for satisfactory intercourse.

Microprocessors would be distributed throughout the bodies of the robot lovers – to control limbs, torso, facial expression, etc., as well as the more intimate parts of the anatomy. We should also remember that modern industrial robots already have a wide range of tactile and other sensors, including sensitive skin (M. Briot at the 1979 International Symposium on Industrial Robots read a paper entitled *'The utilisation of an artificial skin sensor for the identification of solid objects'*). Moreover, computer-based pattern-recognition systems can now even recognize the human face (consider, for example, the Wisard system, being developed at Brunel University). Robot lovers would clearly be skilful enough, though perhaps not moral enough, to remain faithful to their owner.

The robot lover is clearly a practical possibility for the relatively near future – even within the decade (if we are not too fussy) – and we can only imagine what its effects will be. Some observers (for example, Frude, 1983) have portrayed this possibility, though without the anatomical details, in optimistic terms. 'A micro-based doll could have a sexy synthetic voice, peculiar conversational skills and a robotised gymnastic repertoire' (Frude). And it is easy to imagine the advantages that computer capacities would confer on such devices. They would gently stimulate the human lover, noting the response and relying on feedback signals to adjust later performance; and once the mood and tastes of the human being had been detected the robot would never forget, unless it be judged appropriate to the client's wishes that this be done. There are endless possibilities. A man or woman could put down a specification, and a robot lover could be made available to suit. There could be replicas of historical figures, suitably animated and equipped: one could make love with Alexander the Great or with Cleopatra. And all the robots could be rendered soft and warm, with circulating fluid or embedded heaters in the artificial flesh. The dangers are obvious. Here would be the most potent threat to human relationships. If a younger female partner is suddenly seen as sufficiently attractive to induce a married man to leave his wife and family, and often to live in comparative penury, what would be the likely affect of 'specialized surrogates', artificial creatures able to remain permanently healthy, ageless, immensely inventive, completely knowledgeable, flawless in movement and sexual prowess, etc.? If technology once begins to produce such artefacts then human-to-human communication is doomed. Even Frude, ever positive about the technological possibilities, is bound to comment:

> The level of performance which such devices might achieve could indeed lead some people to prefer sensual contact with a soft machine to inter-personal sex and *such a development would clearly challenge and threaten social relationships as we know them* (my italics).

We have already charted some of the dangers of human commitment to computers, and much more could be said. The father of a successful teenage software entrepreneur comments: 'We are very worried about his lack of social life; a computer-science academic criticises the situation in which youngsters are encouraged to spend many hours in their bedrooms without social contact; and a wife struggles to master BASIC in the fruitless struggle to regain her husband's redirected affections.'

The problem is a general one and will intensify as computers proliferate in every human environment. The case of the robot lover shows the extreme end of the human-relations problem: if we can speculate with any cogency about how artificial systems can relate in the most intimate ways to human beings, then the threat is manifest. Again the computer-based robot will be seen as a superior surrogate, able to function in ways that are beyond the capacity of any person. In such a scenario there is only one consequence for intercourse, of whatever kind, between human beings. First there is a desperate rearguard action: jealous and lonely people fight, strive, plea for love; then the few remaining human relationships shrivel and disappear; and finally people adapt to living in isolation, tended only by graceful, brilliant, talented and forever inhuman machines.

This is not all. There is a further dimension to this bizarre picture. It is arguable that computers and robots are emerging life-forms, animate systems based on silicon that will one day supplant all other life on earth. This is a possibility that generates a mixture of ridicule and dread in most human beings. It is a fertile source of fear and phobia.

The Living Computer

People have long speculated that machines might develop into new types of life. Thus Homer (*Iliad*, Book XVIII) hints at the idea: we know about the golden maidens of Hephaestus. Similarly in *Erewhon*, Samuel Butler in 1872 clearly envisaged the emergence of living machines. He was prepared to regard nineteenth-century devices as prototypes of future mechanical life. And Joseph Weizenbaum (1976), less than sympathetic to certain trends in artificial intelligence, is prepared to see computers and robots, appropriately configured, as types of *organisms*, just as the cybernetician James Albus (1981) has noted that it can be argued that 'robots are an evolving life-form'. In this spirit it has been proposed that life-forms may be based on electronic circuits (Dawkins, 1976; Mueller and Mueller, 1983). And even Sir Clive Sinclair has climbed on the bandwagon: in April 1984, at a US congressional meeting, he observed that the science-fiction theme of alternative life-forms would soon become reality ('Silicon will have ended carbon's long monopoly'). There is nothing new in the idea of artificial life-forms.

It is worth glancing at the theme of computer life to see the inherent plausibility of the notion (I have explored the idea in detail elsewhere: Simons, 1983, 1985). If computer-based systems *are* to emerge as an alternative life-form, or a great family of life-forms, then this represents an enormous threat to the hegemony of human beings on earth. For we will see that computers, as increasingly complex systems, have the power to be much superior – in intelligence, imagination, creativity, etc. – to members of the species *Homo sapiens* (see chapter 6).

Two broad considerations bear on the emergence of computer-based life-forms. One concerns the progressive accumulation of life characteristics: the other focuses on whether the chemical metabolisms that characterize earthly life-forms are *essential* to living systems. Taken together, these two considerations suggest the possibility that non-metabolic systems may come to acquire the necessary properties of living things.

In attempting to define life we usually enumerate what are held to be essential qualities. Thus living things, of whatever type, may be expected to grow, move, process incoming information and reproduce. In addition they can probably ingest chemicals to sustain their internal metabolisms, and develop strategies to aid their survival. But it is clear that computers already take in energy, process information, grow, age and involve themselves in the generation of new computers (i.e. reproduce). These various processes and activities can be found in all living things, but vary in character from one species to another, just as the activities of robots may vary from those of human beings. Butler was quick to notice the similarities between machine and animal systems, even in the days when technology was relatively unsophisticated. ('Surely if a machine is able to reproduce another machine systematically, we may say that it has a reproductive system.')

This type of approach suggests that there may be basic life characteristics, ends, to which the various disparate life processes are nothing more than contingent means. For example, James Grier Miller (1978), a highly influential pioneer of systems science, identified nineteen critical subsystems which he regarded as characteristic of all living systems. These various subsystems, which we cannot here explore in detail, are concerned with the tasks of reproducing, processing either energy and information, and processing both. In this systems definition of life – which meets all the requirements of such a definition – there is no assumption that life has to be based on hydrocarbons. If a system can reproduce and handle information and energy in certain ways then *the system may be regarded as living*.

Human beings have a parochial acquaintance with metabolic chemistries, but these only represent the chemical *means* to the behavioural *ends*. It is the on-going activity of the organism – in particular, its development of survival strategies – that gives it its essential life characteristics. But are computers developing survival strategies? How would we begin to recognize such strategies as they emerged? And how would we, as human beings, learn to cope with them? Such strategies would obviously help to define the growing power of the computer; they would relate to the age-old fear of mankind that one day the machines would *take over*. If computers ever learned to adopt modes of behaviour that truly enhanced their place in society, then man would become much less secure in consequence. In such circumstances, we may be tempted to see the computer as an invincible opponent, disposed – as various observers have suggested – to keep people as pets(!), but where the computer was, to all intents and purposes, *omnipotent* (see chapter 6).

The possibility that computers and robots may *come alive* can scarcely be expected to lessen people's anxieties about the development of intelligent machines in the modern age. But this possibility, which can be so plausibly argued, is highly relevant to the emergence of artificial systems as alternative love-objects. Part of our anxiety about sophisticated machines concerns the fact that they behave *as if they are alive:* our apprehension is unlikely to diminish when we learn that artificial systems may actually come to be alive, a notion that has usually been regarded as fictional. Nor will our fears and phobias disappear when we notice that various philosophers, computer scientists and programmers throughout the world are contemplating how computers may be given emotional dispositions, ethical sensitivity and a degree of autonomy (free will) at least equivalent to that in human beings! (See, for example, 'A Mind of its Own?' in chapter 6.)

We may suspect that the living computer may be a highly prized companion, advisor, love-object. But in such circumstances human beings will only rarely be the recipients of *human* affection. We may speculate on how such a development will affect our individual psychologies and our orientation as social animals.

We have seen how intelligent machines can pose a multidimensional threat to human beings in their most intimate relationships. Already spouses are having to compete with computer systems for attention and affection, a situation which in the past has occurred in connection with other types of artefacts but which now has acquired fresh sinister overtones. For one thing, the computer is a remarkably seductive agent. It promises a new world, bounded only by human imagination and human ingenuity; it offers an alluring retreat, an escape from real difficulties, including domestic problems. And this situation is compounded by the fact that computers are beginning to acquire increasingly personal characteristics. But there is an essential paradox at the heart of this emerging situation.

On the one hand, with emphasis on 'user friendly' designs, computer-based systems are adapting to human physical and psychological requirements; but on the other, because computer-based systems are still relatively primitive, human beings themselves are being encouraged to adapt to the current needs of intelligent artefacts. The consequence is that human psychologies are being distorted in the frantic effort to meet computers *on their terms*. And what is compulsion and addiction to one person may also generate fear and apprehension, sometimes in the same person, often in others.

The situation is compounded when it is realized that there *are* ways in which computer systems will evolve to become remarkable friends and lovers. Specifications will be laid down – and computer-based robots will look, talk, behave, 'love' accordingly. But such gadgets will still be artificial, alien, inhuman. For reasons of self-gratification, addiction, escapism, etc., this fact will be ignored by people who learn to depend on intelligent artefacts. And they will be aided in their deliberate lack of perception by the natural human propensity to view things – any things – in animistic or anthropomorphic terms. Intelligent robots will be increasingly perceived as human, affectionate, alive – a development that will be assisted by the remarkable characteristics of the new computer-based systems. In this scenario, with machines replacing people in human affections, there is scope for the greatest disruption in human psychology. It represents perhaps the most grave dehumanizing threat posed to mankind by intelligent machines.

5

The War-Maker

Preamble

Science and technology have always been involved in military affairs. We may assume that David was more in touch with contemporary technology than was Goliath, and all succeeding war-making generations have learned, if not from this example, then from others. The Spartans, for instance, well known for their military prowess, also had a highly developed technology. Their smiths are said to have made the first locks and keys of the modern type. And a recent theory mentioned by Sprague de Camp (1977) suggests that the Spartans owed their success in war to having invented steel or at least to have been the first nation to equip all their troops with steel weapons, at a time when other armies had to make do with weapons made of soft wrought iron or bronze.

Around 400 BC, Dionysios, ruler of Syracuse, was keen to apply contemporary technology to warfare. One aim was to apply new ideas to the development of machines that were already effective in military affairs. Siege engines, for example, were already old at the start of the Golden Age of Greece, but there was always room for improvement. Dionysios gathered together skilled workmen, dividing them into teams, and 'offering great bounties to any who created a supply of arms'. Then, as now, a vast amount of treasure was invested in making rulers and ruling classes as secure as possible by stimulating the manufacture and stockpiling of arms. One of the hired groups invented the military catapult, essentially a large crossbow mounted on a pedestal to fire a six-feet-long arrow. Hence some military historians look to Dionysios as the first ruler to establish ordnance departments and to stimulate the invention of artillery. On occasions he wore a steel vest, but Alexander the Great was the first known warrior to wear an iron helmet.

And so it went on: siege engines, mobile belfries, rams, catapults to project rocks and darts, etc. Such devices evolved through experimental pressures in countless wars in the ancient world and later. The progress of such mechanical contraptions was only diverted or arrested when other sciences developed to the point when they could contribute to the slaughter of human beings. Thus chemists devised gunpowder, castles were rendered obsolete at a stroke, and there was no longer a need for siege engines and rams. The science of explosives stimulated new research into metallurgy, to provide more effective guns and tougher armour. The technologies that stimulated ever greater destruction also sired the production of tough substances that could go some way to resist the explosive onslaughts. In this happy fashion we reached the modern age, in which technology became ever more successful in providing ruling classes with the means of converting living human beings into dead ones. And it was inevitable that computers would contribute to the perfection of means for mass slaughter. It was, after all, in the military womb that the first electronic digital computers were conceived and encouraged to grow.

The Military Stimulus

We have already noted the military involvement in early computer development. The Bletchley code-breaking systems were developed in the Second World War for specific military ends. The ENIAC computer, completed in 1946, was designed to generate artillery firing tables. And even the ubiquitous microprocessor, the effective 'brain' of modern microcomputers and countless other devices, was originally developed by Fairchild for aerospace and defence applications (though the first microprocessor is usually attributed to Intel in 1971). The US Defence Department has listed the Intel 8080 microprocessor as a 'military standard' for procurement purposes. Today some of the largest computer complexes are maintained by military organizations, and military funding stimulates a substantial proportion of all computer development.

Experimental work on new integrated circuit substances and designs is often funded by military departments. As one example, since 1975 the Pentagon has provided at least $6 million to develop integrated circuits based on gallium arsenide, one of the competitors with silicon. We may take it as highly significant that gallium arsenide (GaAs) circuits have high radiation tolerance, a circumstance that is obviously relevant to the possibility of nuclear war (Iversen, 1983). In another estimate the US government, through the Department of Defence and the National Aeronautics and Space Administration, is investing some $100 million in research and development funds to support the work on GaAs circuits. Allan (1983) notes that the 'government's primary focus for GaAs technology is on military applications'.

The armed services are interested in GaAs technology for a variety of computer-based and other military applications. Such technology is deemed relevant to various types of electronic warfare, radar, satellite communications, expendable jammers, and new types of sophisticated radio receivers that could be used in difficult battlefield environments. GaAs signal processors are required by the US Air Force for identification systems and for the joint Air Force-Navy threat-warning facility, a highly computerized system. And GaAs-based circuits are also being developed for 'smart' shells (i.e. shells that can cope with unexpected flight contingencies), antipersonnel radar, miniature communications systems, etc. (projects include: the Electronic Intelligence facility, the Terminally Guided Submissile Seeker, Sense and Destroy Armour, Smart Target Actuated Fire and Forget, and the Multichannel Command Post Radio).

In the modern world, vast funds are being invested in countless military projects. Weizenbaum has quoted a paper circulated to staff by the director of a major US university computer laboratory. Most of the laboratory's research, the director declares, is supported by the US Department of Defence – which is developing ever more destructive weapons that are increasingly *commanded by computers*. Such systems, the director suggests, 'are responsible in large part for the maintenance of what peace and stability there is in the world'. And they are also capable 'of unleashing destruction of a scale that is almost impossible for man to comprehend'.

The Computer Impact

There is a massive, and largely unpredictable, computer impact on military affairs worldwide. This impact has many levels and many dimensions, and in some areas computers are manifestly working against the interests of those individuals and governments who variously design, operate, administer and fund them. For example, a senior researcher at the Washington-based Worldwatch Institute has argued that computer-based technologies are driving the strategic balance of power between the West and the communist countries to a highly unstable state. Thus Daniel Deudney has proposed (in the 1983 report *Whole Earth Security: A Geopolitics of Peace*) that developments such as improved sensory technology, communications technology and the relevant computer-based technologies are destabilizing since they generate undue confidence in the minds of the military planners. The various technologies have created the idea 'that you can have a protracted or limited nuclear war because you can keep tabs on all your dispersed forces'.

Another dimension of the computer impact involves making weapons 'smarter', more able to cope with the difficulties of actual warfare, so vastly increasing the destructive power of computer-based weapons systems. There are, for example, computer systems in the Pershing, Cruise and Trident missiles. Computer-based weapons are now becoming the norm for all the developed countries (see below). And computers are also helping in the *manufacture* of weapons systems. Thus computer-controlled robots, working in conjunction with machine tools, are now making missile fins. In one application two Unimate robots are being used to process the fins through no less than eight separate machining stages (including rough machining, finishing, and the cutting of complex slots). In another munitions application, robots are being used to depalletize empty projectiles: here two robots work in co-operative harmony, allowing flexibility of operation to meet varying national needs and freeing human beings from the hazardous environment of munitions manufacture. Doubtless the robots are also more cost-effective than human workers.

A principal aim of computer-based systems is, according to manufacturers and governments, to increase national security in the military domain. We have already instanced reasons for thinking that the imagined security may be quite illusory, and many other reasons of this sort may be adduced. For example, where a country depends totally on computers for its national security any threat to the continued viability of such computers must have the gravest security implications. Attention was recently focused on this sort of consideration by claims (reported in the *Guardian*, 14 April 1984) of a Liberal MP, Paddy Ashdown, that the USA had access through Ministry of Defence contacts to details of British high-technology exports. It was suggested that the US was using the Cocom agreement, designed to restrict the export of sensitive high technology to Soviet bloc countries, as an instrument for a trade war and not as a security device. An American Defence Department official was even quoted as threatening 'a complete embargo' on any country which refused to observe US Government regulations. 'Since nine out of ten computers in Britain are of American manufacture . . . such an embargo would not only cause havoc in our industry, but would also threaten our national security' (Ashdown). It seems obvious that undue reliance on computer-based systems works against the very purposes the systems were set up to achieve.

It is worth listing, partly by way of summary, some of the ways in which computers are becoming increasingly involved in military matters:

1. Computer-based systems are being used to manufacture munitions of various types. This will allow the more effective use of funds for stockpiling weapons.
2. Computers are being incorporated into more and more weapons. These 'smart' weapons will be more effective in killing both civilians and the members of the (enemy's) armed forces.
3. Computers are being used to facilitate the holding of *war games*, simulated war scenarios used to test the effectiveness of different war-making strategies.
4. Computers are increasingly being involved in the decision-making that determines whether a war will be started or not. The requirement for such an automated facility is directly brought about by the increased effectiveness of new-generation weapons. Missiles, for example, are today so fast and accurate that human beings may not be quick enough to react – so, through 'launch-on-warning' systems, it may be computers that will one day press the button!

We see a progressively developing situation in which computers are taking over all the central military domains. In the forseeable future, computers will be in a position to determine precisely when a war is begun and with precisely which computer-controlled weapons. This does not mean that the computers will necessarily guarantee victory: there are, after all, computers on both sides. What it does mean is that the central choice as to war or peace is gradually being taken out of human hands: *the human race may be plunged into a nuclear inferno in circumstances that human beings never envisaged or intended.*

This perhaps is the most disturbing element in modern computerized society, and it deserves much more public attention than it is currently receiving. Arthur C. Clarke, author of *2001: A Space Odyssey*, has declared that today wars may not start in the minds of men but in the circuits of computers. In such an eventuality, the computer would become the last earthly warmaker of them all.

Computerized Weapons

The development of weapons throughout history has, in one dimension, been represented by an increase in the degree of automation. Consider, for example, the centuries-long evolution from the sling-shot to the modern artillery piece. The aim in each case is to project an object at high velocity to cause damage to property of personnel. With the sling-shot the projectile is supplied with energy by human effort; with modern guns, artillery included, the energy is supplied by chemical reactions. This is an example of the general way in which increased automation is brought to a system: a scientifically controlled process serves to replace human effort – this is as true on the battlefield as in the modern factory.

Jasia Reichardt (1978) illustrated this point by citing the development of the machine gun. In the sixteenth century, machine guns were manual devices requiring great human effort to operate a complicated array of barrels. By the 1880s, with the introduction of the Maxim 'self-acting' machine gun, the required human effort was considerably reduced. And today most sophisticated armies have a variety of guns controlled by computers (sometimes in conjunction with electronic tactical maps). The next stage, already reached with some weaponry, is for the gun (or missile) to fire in a completely autonomous fashion when appropriate incoming control signals are received. This stage is fraught with hazard for mankind (see The Computer War-maker, below).

Modern warfare is being revolutionized by the emerging technologies (what have been dubbed the ETs). There are parallel developments in, for example, computer technology, fuels, armour, explosives, communications, etc. Weapons are more potent, and at the same time more compact and easier to transport from one site to another. Sensor technology is now providing devices that can acquire masses of pertinent information – *which has to be handled by computers* (human beings could not cope with such a volume of information in the critical time available). For this reason, great attention is being given to the progressive automation of command, control and communications (C3). This can be seen as a high-tech development of many of the weapons systems that have emerged in recent years: devices are envisaged, developed and manufactured – and then used for the basis of even more potent systems for mass destruction.

We have long envisaged the use of automation on the battlefield. Many robot scenarios have depicted massive aggressive creatures strutting through a devastated landscape (H. G. Wells, with *The War of the Worlds*, was not the first to imagine that robots might be used for military purposes). In 1939 a robot soldier was shown at the New York Exhibition. This fellow was over nine feet tall, weighed half a ton, and was radio controlled – in the days before there was a single electronic computer in the world. An 18-horsepower motor was used to move its two legs, each equipped with a caterpillar track. The robot's arms wielded clubs, and the device was said to be able to exude asphyxiating gases. We have not seen much of him since. More recently, in the 1980s we have seen the introduction of Odex 1, a robot weighing 370 pounds and standing 6½ feet tall. This fellow, manufactured by the California company Odetics, is intended as the first in a planned family of *functionoids* which could be used for sentry duty, surveillance, law enforcement and many other duties. Odex 1 has six legs and can lift many times its own weight. It (he?) is also equipped to *climb* stairs, changing its posture and gait as necessary. Such robot devices are futuristic, fanciful and of doubtful military value. By contrast there are a host of computer-controlled military systems that are now considered essential for national defence in half the countries of the world.

Computers are being used, for example, to control guns on tanks. The Royal Ordnance Factory at Leeds in 1983 delivered the first Challenger tank with computerized gun to the British Army. One purpose of the computer system is to maintain the aim of the gun, allowing it to continue pointing accurately at targets, even when the tank is moving quickly over rough terrain. An array of sensors is used to monitor wind speed and direction, air temperature and other factors that might adversely affect the flight of a shell. The human gunner uses a laser to measure the range of an enemy tank, whereupon suitable information is fed to the on-board computer. Motors are then automatically instructed to slew the turret and raise the gun barrel to the correct position, so allowing the gun to operate accurately over 2000 metres.

In the same spirit, computers have been recruited to guide Sting Ray, the torpedo currently in service with the British Royal Navy and Air Force. This system, developed by Marconi, has cost approaching £1000 million to develop, and there is some controversy about its effectiveness. The computer-based facility is supposed to analyse sounds picked up by acoustic sensors and to compare them with stored information, allowing a distinction to be made between submarines and other underwater objects and, hopefully, between friendly and hostile craft. We are told that the computer is too bright to be confused by decoys and other countermeasures. Marconi are on record as saying that the Sting Ray scale of investment would be hard to justify in commercial terms.

Marconi have also developed computer-controlled radar for the interceptor version of the Tornado multi-role combat aircraft. In this system, 'well over a dozen' Motorola microprocessors are employed, and the facility is supposed to be able to track more than two-dozen targets simultaneously. It is intended that Tornado will carry radar-directed guided missiles (for example, Sky Flash and Sidewinder). In the absence of comment from Marconi, are we to assume that the millions spent on the Tornado computer systems is money well spent?

Again we may enquire how reliable are the new computer-based military systems. Occasionally we see alarming reports in both the technical and general press about test failures in missiles and aircraft that rely upon silicon chips. For example, early tests of the Cruise missile resulted in some bizarre performance aberrations. Perhaps most alarming of all were the Pentagon revelations of September 1984 . . .

At a much-publicised Pentagon briefing for reporters it was disclosed that millions of Texas Instruments microchips used in modern weapon systems might be faulty. The problem was that some essential test procedures were seemingly not carried out by the company before the chips were released for inclusion in the military systems. Richard DeLauer, the US under-secretary of defence responsible for weapons development, declared: 'Perhaps Texas Instruments employees unilaterally decided to alter some of the acceptance tests or in some cases had even eliminated some of them'.

It is hard to over-estimate the importance of this disclosure. The TI chips were incorporated in thousands of military systems – radars, bombers, early-warning systems, missile-guidance systems, etc. Britain's Chevaline warheads, the successor to Polaris, carry TI chips, as do Cruise missiles. This means that such weapons cannot be assumed to be reliable, if ever they were to be used, and – perhaps even more frighteningly – there is the possibility that faulty chips in radar and satellite systems could give misleading early-warning indications.

We should also appreciate that the revelations about Texas Instruments are not isolated events. In March 1984, the National Semiconductor Corporation was fined £1,300,000 for falsifying tests on silicon chips destined for inclusion in military systems. We are now in the truly horrendous situation that silicon circuits not known for certain to be reliable are now installed in highly-complex weapons systems that could destroy the human race.

There are already many instances of computers used in warfare. In Vietnam, because of falsified reports, computers earned a noxious reputation; and in the Falklands war it seems that computer-controlled defensive measures were no match for offensive computer-controlled Exocets. In April 1984 it was reported the US AC-130 Spectre gunships, equipped with a variety of computer-controlled weapons, were illegally flying over Nicaragua (US denials convinced no-one).

The success of the Exocet missiles in the Falklands conflict only served to draw attention to the relevance of high technology to modern weaponry. The British destroyer, HMS Sheffield, sunk by an Exocet on 4th May 1982, was a highly-rated ship built at a cost of about £28 million 10 years ago. If such a ship could be sunk by a 'smart' missile then it demonstrated the effectiveness of computerized guidance systems for such a purpose. We were soon reminded that Exocet was only one of many missiles that carried on-board computers to provide a degree of local 'intelligence'. (The Argentines fired six Exocet missiles and four of them found a target.)

Today Exocet is seen as characteristic of modern antiship missiles. Other such devices are the Gabriel Mk III (Israel), the Harpoon RGM-84A (ISA), the Tomahawk BGM-109 (USA), the Styx SS-N-2C (USSR), and the Kitchen AS-4 (USSR). Such missiles store data in their memories, and process changing trajectory information in order to home in on a target. The so-called 'smart' missiles are commonplace in the arsenals of the world.

It is now conventional for computers to be incorporated into the design of weapons, whether the weapons are to be used on land, in the air or at sea. The idea is that missiles — for example, Cruise — will be able to cope with environmental or other variations in the operating situation. Computers effectively provide missiles, shells, torpedoes, etc. with intelligent pilots, goal-seeking agents that are happily expendable. Unfortunately, whichever side you are on, the enemy has much the same idea. Vast resources are invested in high-tech military systems — *to achieve diminished security!*

Playing War Games

Computers are very good at *pretending*, at simulating real events. In some sense this represents a type of computer imagination: intelligent machines can play around with possibilities that mirror or mimic objects and activities in the world. This facility is particularly useful for matters relating to war, since computers can have 'pretend' battles that do not involve the loss of personnel or treasure. Here military personnel can put forward strategic options, run the computer, and see what happens. Often, however, the results are difficult to interpret and, in any case, are derived from simplistic or questionable assumptions.

At the simplest level, computer simulators can be used to train staff to fly aircraft, drive tanks, etc.: an array of dials, gauges, switches and screens is employed to control the simulations – mistakes involve loss of dignity rather than loss of life. For example, the Purdy Machinery company in the UK has developed optical probe devices as components of the Singer simulation system for the training of tank gunners and tank drivers. The probes feed a servo-controlled, closed-circuit television system to relay information from a simulated terrain (a scale model is provided of suitable territory) to the trainee driver. The system can be used for other fighting vehicles, including aircraft. One aim is to use many different colours to achieve a high degree of realism on the screen displays, but how realistic in fact *are* such simulations? Is there a smoke-laden atmosphere, mutilated corpses, all the terribly anxiety about the possibility of sudden death, a nuclear explosion or two? It is highly significant that simulation for war purposes can only be evaluated after the war has taken place. It may be that some people would welcome the experiment. Most of us would not.

We may be disturbed at the extent to which modern high-tech companies are involved in the armaments industry, but we are rarely concerned about the many electronics firms that provide gadgets to kill pretend people. Weston Simfire of Enfield, for instance, spends much of its time researching how to simulate gunnery systems. The company is best known for its Simfics tank gunnery simulation system used to mimic the firing of shells from a Chieftain tank. Here a pulse from a gallium arsenide (GaAs) laser in the gun barrel simulates an actual firing, and the principle is being extended to apply to other guns and missiles. In one application, a laser-based system is used for infantry battle training: soldiers fit a laser emitter to the barrels of their rifles and machine guns, and wear a harness which distributes fifteen laser detectors about their bodies. When a laser pulse hits a detector in a simulated battlefield encounter, the soldier obligingly stops fighting and pretends to be dead: he is informed of his demise by a horn that sounds on the harness. In 1984 the Centronics company of Croydon was also developing this type of system for the British Army.

Simfire claims all sorts of advantages for its infantry battle simulators. For example, the equipment modules are small and when fastened to rifles do not affect their balance or feel. When a blank round is fired, the laser-pulse projector is automatically operated and has a range of up to 1100 metres. Near misses as well as direct hits are recorded so that the soldiers have some indication of the accuracy of their fire. This is accomplished by firing pulses of different cross-sectional areas: a continuous horn sound signals a direct hit; a brief blast, a near miss.

Another new development is a family of modules which Simfire reckons can be programmed to simulate the behaviour of every anti-tank, direct-fire missile system in the Western world. The various modules were developed from the Simlan simulator for the British/French/German Milan anti-tank weapon. One objective here is to cope with the complexity of a tank battle. In Simlan and the more sophisticated modules the laser projector has a range of more than 2000 metres and can be fitted into the normal firing tube. When a tank detects a laser pulse, simulating a direct hit, a smoke canister on the tank is set off and the vehicle may be immobilized. On-board computer-based systems estimate the effectiveness of near misses: should they be considered kills or near misses?

The use of lasers in gun barrels and computer-controlled detectors on tanks represents a relatively low-level degree of simulation. It is necessarily constrained by the availability of actual tanks, and only involves the 'killing' of small numbers of military personnel. But military planners have always been ambitious: why only kill a few tank drivers when you can effectively slaughter millions of human beings?

In a 1982 scenario the British Home Office was accused of falsifying the results to reduce the expected number of civilian deaths in the event of nuclear war from the anticipated 29 million to a mere 3 million. In his book *War Plan UK*, Duncan Campbell (1984) discusses extracts from the scenario of 'Hard Rock', as well as details from two earlier exercises ('Scrum Half' and 'Square Leg'). It is suggested that Home Office personnel and military planners misleadingly reduced the scale of an imagined Soviet attack in order to improve morale among civil-defense officials. Thus 'Hard Rock' reduced the anticipated number of Soviet missiles from 130 to a mere 54 (with the power of 48½ megatons, 3000 times the power of the Hiroshima and Nagasaki atomic bombs). Campbell suggests, with good grounds, that the scenario is unrealistic and that the actual war would be much worse, and he quotes a computer analysis showing that the 'Square Leg' nuclear strikes would have killed no less than 29 million people in the UK.

A US publication, the *Nuclear Weapons Data Book*, published in 1983 by Ballinger for the Washington-based National Resources Defence Council, gives the sorts of statistical information about nuclear weaponry that can be used to feed computer-controlled war-gaming exercises. Desmond Ball, a researcher at the Strategic and Defence Studies Centre, at the Australian National University, has published wide-ranging information of this sort. Thus he points out that there are more than 40,000 potential targets in current US strategic targeting plans. These include the Soviet nuclear forces (about 2000 targets), around 20,000 other military targets, the Soviet military and political leadership centres (3000 targets), and about 15,000 economic and industrial targets. In one cited official computer study – in which, significantly, it is assumed that the US strategic weapons are launched before any Soviet weapons explode in the USA – it is calculated that about 8700 targets would be destroyed in the USSR.

The computer nuclear war games tend to disguise the likelihood of civilian casualties, though many of the targets are in or near cities. The Soviet Union has nearly 1000 cities with populations of about 25,000 each, and the US war plans anticipate the destruction of at least 80 per cent of these cities. In addition it is expected that the 200 largest Soviet cities will be *totally* destroyed. Doubtless the Soviet military planners contemplate analogue scenarios for the destruction of the USA.

The war-planning game, impossible today without computers, is now an immensely complicated affair. Apart from the vast number of potential targets and the constantly shifting levels of weaponry on both sides, there are countless war-waging scenarios that can be considered. Which side strikes first? With precisely what strategy? Is there a 'controlled escalation' and 'flexible response'? How much destruction can be 'absorbed' if the other side strikes first? How long will a nuclear war last? Who will win? What, exactly, is to count as victory?

In such a convoluted and complex situation there are a host of terrifying considerations. How accurate are the assumptions on which the computer war games are based? Can we trust the complicated computer systems to deliver the goods? (See The Computer War-maker, below). In fact the sheer scale of the computational exercise makes most war-gaming an absurdly unrealistic approach. In any scenario, the variables are so many – involving, as they do, the immensely complicated statistics for weaponry and personnel, the vagaries of human decision-making, the largely unpredictable impact of weather conditions and other shifting environmental factors, the impact of early nuclear explosions on communications networks worldwide, etc. – that any attempted computational exercise quickly runs into what mathematicians call the 'combinatorial explosion', i.e. there are too many options to be computed, and compromises and approximations have to be made (in artificial intelligence, for example, 'heuristic' methods are being evolved to overcome the difficulties involved in the combinatorial explosion but such methods are rudimentary).

It has often been pointed out that computer-based war games are based on unrealistic expectations: for example, that the command, control and communications systems will survive long enough to cope with the complex targeting plans and the controlled escalation of the conflict. In fact there are good grounds for thinking that initial nuclear bursts will totally disrupt (for example) satellite communications which are likely to be involved in the targeting of Trident and other missiles. Experts like Desmond Ball have questioned the communications-survival assumption and many other assumptions that are supposed to underpin the war-game conclusions. And there are also a host of technical problems that render war games totally untrustworthy. For example, there is still controversy in the highly mathematical gaming theory upon which war-game strategies are based; there are crucial imponderables concerning the other 'player' in the 'game'; and there are disturbing unpredictabilities in the complex of computer programs that are used to compute war-game scenarios (see The Computer War-Maker, below).

There are also immense psychological hazards in the war-gaming approach. Practitioners are encouraged in various modes of distorted and delusional thinking. On the one hand, quite erroneously, they assume that their complex computer simulations are accurate reflections of reality; and, on the other hand, the simulations are manifestly purged of all the unpleasant human connotations – such as shrivelled corpses and flesh rotting with radiation sickness. And, just as with the hackers, there are inevitable delusions of grandeur. The computer planners see themselves playing a *literal* game, manipulating vast resources to defeat the embodiment of evil, the depersonalized enemy. But this is a totally artificial and unrealistic situation. The planners are not effectively constrained by appropriate contact with reality. Their symbols, charts and displays are not concerned, in any immediate psychological sense, with human beings. They are focused on resources to be deployed, goals to be achieved, gaming decisions to be taken, etc. This can only be seen as an appallingly dehumanizing activity. Millions of human beings – ordinary people struggling to cope with life's problems, the sick in hospitals, young lovers, failing geriatrics, babes in arms – are reduced to symbols on a screen, markers that can be obliterated when this or that program is called up. It has long been pointed out that it is much easier to kill a *dehumanized* person – so we invent diminishing and derogatory labels ('huns', 'krauts', 'nip', 'argies', 'gooks'). But the war-gaming computer relies upon the most diminishing symbols of all: flesh-and-blood human beings are reduced to nothing more than a pattern of pulses in a solid-state memory.

The war-gaming approach to military planning is thus subject to many crucial objections. These are worth emphasizing:

1. Gaming theory is contentious, disputable and unreliable in many particulars and at many levels.
2. War games represent highly simplified representations of reality. They are parodies of what it would be like to be involved in a real nuclear conflagration. They are thus highly misleading.
3. War games also rely upon highly questionable assumptions which, in themselves, are highly complex and not amenable to adequate manipulation in formal symbolic systems.
4. The representation of human beings in war-game scenarios is a grossly dehumanizing process. It completely diminishes the intended victims of nuclear activity, making them mere signs on a video display that can be obliterated at will.
5. The involvement in war-game scenarios is dehumanizing for the participants. Their values become distorted, they ignore the human relevance of their exercises, and they develop an exaggerated view of their own powers (delusions of grandeur, the hacker syndrome).
6. Complex interacting programs are capable of behaving in incomprehensible and unpredictable ways. Even if the war-game assumptions were sound and comprehensive, the game outcomes could not be trusted.

It is not surprising, when so much can be said, that there is concerned reaction amongst technologists and other people against the use of computers for war-planning exercises: not everyone is prepared to abandon contact with ethical values and reality.

There are cases on record where individuals have resigned from computer-based military systems. Hall (1984), for example, instances the case of Dave Caulkins who left his job with the Pentagon's Minuteman missile programme 'for moral reasons' after which he helped to set up a computer conferencing system in California to encourage discussion about arms control and disarmament. Similarly, consultant Arthur Fink has founded a Centre for Appropriate Computing in Wilton, New Hampshire, to stimulate debate among 'those who use or are touched by computer technology'. Fink has observed: 'We should all affirm that we face ethical question in our industry.' And High Technology Professionals for Peace (HTPFP) opened an employment agency in Boston in 1982 to find non-military-related jobs for computer, engineering and scientific staff. Dr Severo Ornstein, a computer scientist at Xerox, has emphasized that as defence systems increase in complexity they need more computer processing. ('Larger and larger pieces of the decision-making apparatus get turned over to computer systems. The more one turns over to machines, the more one comes vulnerable to their fallibility.') One substantial area of concern is the use of computers in war-gaming applications. Hall: 'High-tech weapons could turn out to be a gossamer Maginot Line made of blueprints and scientific ideas *that could never work in the real world*' (my italics).

The successful film *War Games*, in which a young computer enthusiast keys in to a military defence network, has been applauded by many computer specialists as a realistic scenario (in fact the screenwriters Walter Parkes and Larry Lasker researched the US strategic nuclear weapons establishment for two years). Parkes has commented: 'We didn't know that the movie would have an anti-nuclear script when we started out. When it comes out of a process like the one that we went through . . . I think it reflects a truer sense . . . You want to believe that nuclear defence is in good hands; however, the more we looked into it, *the more we realised that nobody is in control*' (my italics). In *War Games*, a high-school student is innocently playing computer games when he inadvertently breaks into a computer system (the WOPR, War Operation Planned Response) and brings the world to the brink of nuclear disaster. It is easy to see why the US authorities are sufficiently nervous to encourage antihacker legislation!

In 1984 a series of events occurred which made the *War Games* fantasy seem even more plausible (report in *Financial Guardian*, 22 March 1984). Two teenage hackers managed to 'break in' to the secret ARPA computer network, the electronic data exchange of the Pentagon's Advanced Research Projects Agency. This led to an electronic chase that crossed the US continent to the Norwegian Telecommunications Agency, and included visits to NORAD, the North American Air Defence headquarters in a deep bunker in Omaha, Nebraska ('Such details gave the caper an uncomfortable similarity to the plot of *War Games*'). In this actual case, the pursuit of the hackers went on in the computers of such organizations as Stanford Research International, the Rand Corporation, the National Research Laboratory, two east-coast defence contractors, two scientific research firms and several universities! In due course, two Los Angeles teenagers, Kevin Poulsen and Ron Austin, were arrested in their homes by six armed law-enforcement officers. The boys had cracked the massive secret network using two microcomputers (a VIC-20 and a TRS-80), neither costing more than £140.

This case was relatively unimportant from a national security point of view. No secrets were lost and there was never any prospect of an unintended launch of a Third World War holocaust (the press dubbed the case 'the computer kids' War Games caper'). But what was revealed was the glaring fragility of a key national computer network. If the vulnerability of such a system allowed such relatively easy penetration, what other surprises was the military establishment in for? Questions were quickly asked about the comprehensibility of complex computer configurations, and many of the answers were far from reassuring. The Poulsen/Austin affair merely underlined many of the anxieties that were beginning to surface about the increasing role of computers in national defence networks.

The use by military planners of computer-based systems for war-gaming and related activities is stimulating a high degree of apprehension in many quarters, but at least with war-gaming the human being is still an involved agent of decision-making: people may choose wrongly, influenced by simplistic criteria, and in a distorted and dehumanized fashion – but they are still there. What is even more alarming is the increasingly realistic possibility that human beings will be totally excluded from the decision-making loop, *that the computer will become the sole war-maker!*

The Computer War-Maker

People have often worried that computers may cause a nuclear war that no-one intended, and such anxieties are not helped by headlines such as 'The computer that keeps declaring war' (*The Sunday Times*, 22 June 1980). We learn that a small piece of silicon the size of a coin set off a false alarm of a missile attack on the United States on 3 June 1980. This single faulty component alerted the entire North American defence command, and this event was not the only one of its kind. In the late 1970s and early 1980s many military experts were worried by the number of failures occurring in the Worldwide Military Command and Control System (known as Wimex). John Bradley, the former chief test engineer on the computer network, has been reported as saying that the system is so unreliable that senior military officials no longer trust it. He reckons that there are ten false alerts for every one that the press hears about.

Wimex, which, by the early 1980s, was 10 years out-of-date, has been described as slow and inaccurate. In has interpreted a rolling bank of fog and a flock of geese as missile attacks, and one estimate suggests that the system fails about once every 35 minutes. The suggestion is that if Wimex ever *did* detect a real missile attack then no-one would believe it. In 1976 General Alexander Haig declared, in a memo to the joint chiefs of staff in Washington, that Wimex 'is generally considered to be inefficient and approaching obsolescence'. Yet years later the complex and unreliable system was still expected to provide the crucial information that an American President would need to declare war on the Soviet Union. It is worth exploring in a little more detail some of the circumstances surrounding the Wimex configuration.

Wimex is at the heart of the US command and control capability. The European Command (EUCOM) and each of its sub-commands is equipped with a Wimex computer, a Honeywell 6000 Series machine, designed and built in the 1960s. The aim is for the various computers to pass information between the military commands and the National Command Authority headed by (or identified with) the American President. But the computer configuration appears not to have worked well. In the words of one writer (Campbell, 1984), 'the Wimex network appears to have been an unmitigated disaster'.

The system began operation in the mid-1970s, but for periods running into months and even years an hour's continuous operation was a rarity – breakdowns were so common. Two Wimex computers began operation at the North American Air Defense (NORAD) headquarters in Colorado in September 1979 – and within 9 months the US nuclear forces around the world had been accidentally put on war alert no less than three times. In these circumstances, aircraft took to the air and preparations were begun to launch missiles. The *Washington Post* (14 August 1983) reported that one missile launch-crew member telephoned his wife and told her to head for Canada; another strapped on a gun and resolved to 'die like a soldier'; and no less than thirteen of seventeen crews at the Titan missile base in Kansas failed to obey orders. Worldwide nuclear alerts had been caused by loading a wrong tape onto a computer and, later, by the failure of a $20 silicon chip!

One NORAD false alarm occurred in November 1979 when a war-game simulation tape was loaded into a computer. Soon air-defence fighters were in the air over Missouri, Oregon and British Columbia. The UK early-warning system at Fylingdales, Yorkshire, was alerted, and an official later observed that 'things got very tense'.

The US General Accounting Office (GAO), a government budgetary watchdog, noted that by 1980 the Pentagon had spent $1 billion on Wimex in an attempt to make the computers work as intended. It emerged that this attempt was futile and the GAO report (LCD80-22, 14 December 1979) concluded that the Wimex system: was not reliable; was not responsive to national or local level requirements; could not transfer data and information efficiently; impaired a commander's operational back-up capability. In particular, Wimex had not achieved one of its central purposes – to bring a degree of standardization to

158 different computer systems employed in military commands. It was recognized that US command and control failures had resulted, in the 1960s, in costly humiliations for the United States (for example, in the attacks by Israel and North Korean forces on the *Liberty* and *Pueblo* intelligence ships). But the Wimex system did not improve matters. For instance, in a 1977 command exercise the US Joint Chiefs of Staff found that at four (out of six) Wimex locations, 62 per cent of computer operations went wrong. This did not stop the Wimex Intercomputer Network (WIN), though clearly unstable and unreliable, being classified as 'operational' – and programmers struggled to write 'patch' programs to cope with known errors, often adding new faults in the process (see also The Incomprehensible Computer, below).

By June 1980 we were treated to another false alert: a faulty chip in a NORAD system sent out random numbers indicating a Soviet missile attack. Again bombers and tankers actually started their engines and waited to take off; in Hawaii, aircraft became airborne. Three days later, NORAD technicians set off another false alarm, claiming that this was a deliberate action but failing to warn Strategic Air Command – which again went on alert. When an effort was made to test the Wimex system in November 1980, the computers malfunctioned for a 12-hour period. Yet this is the system upon which military planners are increasingly forced to rely.

However, it is also sigificant that the computer involvement in war-making is not confined to possible confrontations between the USA and the USSR. Roland Perry has described (in *Computing*, 24 May 1984) how computer facilities helped the 1983 invasion of Grenada by US forces. Perry: 'The whole operation from invasion to President Reagan's TV announcement ("We got there just in time") was monitored and guided by the most advanced war computer network ever designed.' Dr Richard Beal had developed a computerized Crisis Management Centre which was able to collect and manipulate vast amounts of information to aid presidential decision making at times of crisis. It is suggested that: 'Beal's computer system may well have accelerated the US's "Lone Ranger" mentality in handling wars.' Again we see the computer stimulating the urge to military adventure: the aggressive impulse receives the ultimate technological sanction – *that the computer approves such and such a course of action.*

The involvement of the computer in small local wars (Grenada, Nicaragua, the Falklands, etc.) has obvious implications for world peace. Any local aggression may be interpreted by a super-power as an 'unacceptable' hostility – with consequences for the world. And it is important to realize that the possibility of a computer malfunction – whether a component fault or erroneous advice generated by increasingly incomprehensible software – has many disturbing implications.

The possibility of a computer fault in a major military system has a number of destabilizing effects. It is not only that inaccurate information may cause military and political leaders to launch nuclear missiles against an enemy. It is also true that the opposite side, aware of the possibility of such a computer malfunction in the equipment of its adversary, may be tempted to launch a pre-emptive first strike before a mistaken attack can be made on its own territory. In short, if computer unreliability means that nuclear war is inevitable, then each side has a great incentive to be the first to start it. At the time when Wimex went fully operational, a report by the US Defence Communication Agency was complaining of 'repeated system failure, failure during electrical storms or when power systems are subject to voltage and frequency fluctuations'.

The idea that faulty silicon chips could cause a war is bad enough, but there is more. There is even the possibility that computers that are functioning perfectly well could take the decision to launch nuclear missiles at the enemy – in the absence of any enemy action that would justify such a decision. Joseph Weizenbaum was one of the first to realize that computers were being allowed a judgemental role in war situations. He wrote (in 1976) that 'During the Vietnam war, *computers operated by officers who had not the slightest idea of what went on inside their machines effectively chose which hamlets were to be bombed*' (my italics). What was happening was that computers, supplied with highly complex software (that was probably not fully understood by *any* human being), were being expected to control important tactical aspects of the war. When we realise that this approach has now been extended to the broad strategic questions of whether to launch nuclear missiles we can see that the situation is nothing less than horrendous.

In 1983 it was reported (*New Scientist*, 21 April 1983) that specialists were researching how computers could take the place of generals on the battlefield. Ed Taylor, of TRW Defence Systems in California, has remarked that the *main problem* of fighting a modern was is that 'you have good generals and dumb generals', and he believes that research should be conducted to enable computers to make the right tactical decisions as consistently as the top 10 per cent of generals. TRW delivered a feasibility study to the Pentagon in 1983 indicating how such research should proceed. For example, it would be necessary to observe generals' decisions in war games – those wonderful war games! – to see which commanders made the best decisions and how these decisions varied from poor ones. Then this 'judgemental ability' could be put into a computer.

This sort of approach requires that the human being be excluded from the decision-making loop. Once the computer has been set up and equipped to think on its own, so the theory runs, then human beings would only delay matters. Decisions using masses of new data may have to be taken in thousandths of a second, and human beings are just not equipped for this level of mental performance. It is this sort of consideration that is giving great impetus to the development of 'launch-on-warning' systems. Here early warning satellites would supposedly detect hostile missiles as soon as they were launched by detecting the infra-red radiation from the missile plumes. Signals would then be transmitted to the computers controlling the firing of the missiles in the country being attacked. As soon as the appropriate signals were received the missiles would be launched: there would be no way to recall them if an error was then discovered, and impact would take place within minutes (today's Pershing II missiles have a flight time of about 10 minutes to the USSR). This means that *the nuclear holocaust could be initiated by computers without any human decision having been taken.* Not for nothing has this possibility been dubbed the 'ultimate madness'. There can be no doubt that launch-on-warning systems are likely to be deployed in the years to come, and that this development will dramatically increase the possibility of nuclear war by accident.

There are in fact startling reasons why increased reliance on computer systems for military decision-making are bound to generate greater instability and insecurity in national and international defence arrangements. It is important to realise what is happening with complex military computer systems. Again Weizenbaum has pointed to one of the central difficulties:

computer systems are now becoming so complicated that no-one can understand them. In the 'Voices' debate on Channel 4 television (14 March 1984), Weizenbaum emphasized that the large computer systems now operating for military and other purposes are not just uncomprehended but are *'incomprehensible in principle'*. There are various reasons why this is happening, and many of them have to do with the nature of computer programs.

The Incomprehensible Computer

All computer programs comprise sequences of coded instructions written so that the computer will carry out intended tasks, but there are immense variations in complexity from one computer program to another. Moreover great numbers of programs can be linked together – as they are in the vast military systems – to perform different, but equally essential, tasks. A small commercial program (for example, one required for a video game) is likely to comprise a few hundred lines of code, and smaller programs that this can be used for various purposes. However, in the largest computer systems there may well be thousands of co-operating programs comprising, in all, hundreds of thousands of lines of code.

None of the large computer systems have been programmed by one solitary individual: instead they have relied on the team effort of hundreds of programmers, all devoted to particular software modules. Some programmers take care to document their work, explaining the various coded sections; other programmers are less scrupulous. Moreover programmers move on, taking up work with other organizations or being assigned other projects within the same organization. The upshot is that the largest software systems grow in an uncontrolled, increasingly incomprehensible, fashion. If a problem arises, a new piece of program is written as an immediate technological 'fix': it may solve the problem in the short term, but its long-term effects on the established programs are unknown and totally unpredictable. Hence the largest computer software systems evolve in a disorganized fashion, particular programmers understanding bits here and bits there, but no-one understanding the system as a whole. It is worth citing an observation made by Barr and Feigenbaum (1981) in the prestigious *Handbook of*

Artificial Intelligence (Volume 1, p.149). In highlighting the complicated interdependence of procedures in a large program, they note that a change to one procedure, so that it will work with another, may cause the first procedure not to function properly when it is called by a third. Thus, 'in order to modify a large system successfully, the programmer must understand the interactions of all of its pieces, *which can become an impossibly difficult task*' (my italics).

What this means is that complicated programs may work in ways that we cannot understand and will never understand. With each new addition of software and each new program change the program becomes ever more remote from human comprehension. It is nothing less than irresponsible folly for human beings to entrust the safety of nations – even the safety of the human race – to incomprehensible computer systems. Yet this is exactly what is happening.

This chapter has surveyed the role of the computer in warplaning and war-making. We find the computer increasingly involved in weapons themselves, in influencing the thinking of military planners, and in the crucial decision-making process. Through simulation techniques, computers can be used to train soldiers and other personnel, and to investigate competing strategies in 'imaginary' wars. (Using a different type of simulation, a plastic robot is being used at the Brookhaven National Laboratory in the US to monitor radiation doses. The device is said to have similar radiation absorption properties to those of a human being.) In weaponry, artefacts are being equipped with local 'intelligence' to enable them to function more effectively in battlefield conditions – and we have noted the paradox in this development. Both offensive and defensive systems are being provided with computer intelligence, and warfare is increasingly being perpetrated by 'smart' systems with different goals. The Falklands is a classic case of a conflict with computers on both sides.

We have also profiled the impact of war-gaming on human participants (whether military planners or intended victims), indicating various dehumanizing consequences and emphasizing the distorting effects of such practices on our perception of the world. And most significant of all, we have indicated how crucial decision-making is being left to computer systems that are quite incomprehensible to all the people who are supposed to control their operations. Modern computer systems are too complex to be understood by human beings, and as we add every day to this incomprehensible complexity our dependence on computer systems grows deeper. Inexorably we are being sucked into a situation of having to rely, in all the crucial areas of living, on artificial systems that we cannot comprehend. This must surely represent what will emerge as the ultimate victory of the machine over *Homo sapiens*. What is happening in the military sphere is happening in all other walks of life, but it is perhaps in the military area that the encroachment by machine intelligence is most disturbing.

6

The Omnipotent Machine

Preamble

Many people have worried that one day computers and computer-based systems will evolve beyond human control. It is common for people to express an anxiety that intelligent computers and robots may ultimately take over the world and destroy or enslave mankind. This anxiety takes many forms. Sometimes it is reflected in an awareness of the diminished status of human beings in man/computer systems. Thus an article making a plea for better systems design in process control plant is entitled 'Don't forget the operator: he's only human' (*Electrical Review*, 20 March 1981). Here we find a reiteration of the point made in the last chapter, that human beings are becoming detached from the process, with more and more responsibility being assigned to the computer. When something goes wrong, 'the operator is unable to cope and the results can be catastrophic'.

Another related concern, already considered, is that human beings may progressively lose control of computer systems. Hence an article in *New Scientist* (17 January 1980) headed 'Computers that learn could lead to disaster'. Here Donald Michie, agreeing for once with Weizenbaum, is quoted as saying that artificial-intelligence (AI) systems could lead society into a 'technological black hole' in which human beings would not be able to understand the reasoning behind computer decisions in crucial social and scientific areas. And yet other anxieties focus on how computers may develop their own objectives and goals, unknown to human beings, and how such goals may be pursued even if they ran counter to human interest. It is even possible that computers may co-operate with each other, using existing networks, to develop such behavioural modes. Thus Edward Fredkin (quoted in McCorduck, 1979) can comment ominously, 'when they can communicate they can conspire'.

Underlying such fears and phobias is an awareness of the extraordinary power of the modern digital computer. Even the grotesquely inefficient first-generation machines, developed immediately after the Second World War, could carry out 20,000 operations a second and exhibit a variety of problem-solving and decision-making abilities. Today, with this sort of computer power magnified a hundred-fold and at the same time crammed into silicon-based systems the size of a thumbnail, it is easy to see why such remarkable artefacts can stimulate both awe and apprehension. And we do well to remember that not all computers have shrunk to the size of a suitcase or a matchbox. There are still large computer configurations, in some cases covering acres of land, where the density of computer circuits is the same as in the home micro but where the total processing power is vastly greater. It is envisaged that there will be computers designed and functioning, before the end of the decade, that will be able to conduct dozens of conversations at the same time, while processing other computational tasks at the rate of 1000 million operations every second.

It is partly the remarkable speed of the modern computer that facilitates its awesome performance. I well remember how this speed of operation was graphically portrayed by one scientific observer. Imagine, he said, two computers conversing with each other over a period. They are then asked by a human being what they are talking about, and *in the time he takes to pose the question, the two computers have exchanged more words than the sum total of all the words exchanged by human beings since homo sapiens first appeared on earth 2 or 3 million years ago.* Suppose that the two computers are benevolent: they wish to humour the halting creature that has chosen to interrupt their duologue. How are they to respond? How can they convey the essence of even a million million words in terms that will be comprehensible to a mere person? They are likely to conclude that it would be a waste of time to try!

We have seen that the human anxiety about machine systems runs through all human history. It is reflected in myth and legend, in the superstitious of the early Christian fathers, and in much subsequent philosophy and literature. But in this tradition the machine was only rarely conceived as *intelligent*. If stupid, obedient machines could stimulate such a weight of dread, it is scarcely surprising that *intelligent* machines will generate a new level of apprehension. And the prospect that such devices will almost certainly outstrip human mental capabilities has been seen as doubly disturbing. Machines have always out-performed human beings: this was their central *raison d'être*; intelligent machines have for some years outstripped mere mortals (see The Artificial Expert, below); and now we face the prospect that machine intelligence will develop at a rapid rate, and that we may not always be able to chart its course. We will not be able to draw clear theoretical lines around such prodigious machine competence. A computer so conceived will appear to human beings as, to all intents and purposes, *omnipotent*. Throughout history, people have never demanded full empirical evidence to justify their ascriptons of omnipotence (usually to a deity): it was enough that the omnipotent agent so far outstripped human capabilities and understanding that its competence could not be constrained by human imagination. In this sense, and perhaps not only in this sense, *the computer of tomorrow will be omnipotent*. It will be enough that the computer will be able to do this, that and the other – that we can comprehend – superlatively well, and that we will be unable to describe or understand *all* that the computer can do.

In such a scenario we will be totally dependent upon the machine. The old superstitious myths of human dependence on an unreal deity will have been realized in the new secular apocalypse. And, as in the old irrational creeds, *awe* and *fear* will be words on the same lips (compare with *love of God* and *fear of God*, both supposed to co-exist in the same heart). Perhaps we have good cause to be apprehensive about the vast new intelligence being generated in our midst. Lenin once said that the capitalist will sell you the rope to hang him (the capitalist). In the same way, we are striving with all our powers to generate the intelligent systems that may subvert all our human goals.

Only a Machine?

When confronted with the prospect of machine intelligence, people often try to reassure themselves. There are various ways in which this is done. One of the most common of these is well illustrated by an interview with Michael Crichton (author of *The Andromeda Strain* and *The Terminal Man*), as reported in the journal *Infosystems* (March 1984). In the non-fictional *Electronic Life – How to Think About Computers*, he strives to convince a cyberphobic public that computers are not bad or complicated and that they certainly are not out of control – yet. Here it is suggested that people are uneasy about computers because they forget that computers are just machines – perhaps different sorts of machines to the washer or the automobile – but mere machines none the less. But then Crichton echoes some of the anxieties that are already being voiced elsewhere (in connection with the prospect of a 'judgemental role' for intelligent machines): 'It's a terrible idea to have computers serve as judges or psychiatrists. When you learn more about computers, you realise what a mess it would be.'

The *'mere machine'* argument is frequently rehearsed – but, alas, it is easily refuted. One has simply to ask – what is a human being, if not a machine or system of remarkable powers and complexity? If it diminishes computers to dub them *mere machines*, then human beings can be equally diminished by using the same argument, *mutatis mutandis*, in a different context. What the advocates of the mere-machine argument fail to remember is that they are unduly influenced by a prescientific tradition, by (for example) 'substance metaphysics' which postulated the existence of various mythical stuffs out of which bodies, minds and spirits could be composed at the whim of a divine architect. Today there are subtantial reasons – in cybernetics, neurophysiology, biochemistry, systems theory, etc. – for thinking that *mind* (and *spirit*, if we wish to retain the word) is a function of *brain organization and behaviour*. The corollary, for our immediate purposes, is that people – like computers – can be totally defined in terms of their functional components. In this sense, human beings are machines, interested in survival, purpose, emotional fulfilment, etc., but machines none the less. We will not escape from computer fear and phobia by resorting to the 'mere-machine' argument.

Another defensive ploy is to diminish computers and robots by caricaturing their intelligence. And so we hear that computers are nothing more than *'high-speed idiots'*, or that robots are 'only as smart as a clever grasshopper' (*Computing*, 11 November 1982). Some *'idiot'* that can draw a game of chess with world champion Karpov (as did the Mephisto III program) or know more high mathematics than any single human being (as does the MACSYMA expert system)! In fact we cannot take much comfort in the 'idiot theory' of machine intelligence: in several-dozen specific domains computers are already vastly cleverer than all but a very small number of human beings. Computers are evolving a spectrum of intelligent abilities, sometimes in ways that we do not understand. This is an empirical circumstance that would generate a more widespread apprehension if people were more aware of the nature of computer evolution.

The character of machine development has been explored in various ways. Butler had a stab at it in *Erewhon*, but compared with the modern specialist he was ignorant of technology. More recent efforts have drawn on what is known of both human evolution and the development of artefacts; and sometimes there is specific focus on the evolution of computers. In an intriguing article, Rauzino (1982) suggests how an understanding of the human brain hemispheres can give pointers as to the nature of computer evolution. We cannot here explore his arguments in detail: it is enough to remark that he sees it as quite understandable that computers should today have their current natures. Modern computer logic is more akin to left-brain functioning than right (the left brain hemisphere is concerned with rational argument, whereas the right is involved with intuition, creativity, etc.). In short, the implication is that computers will come to evolve right-brain characteristics when they have developed their left-brain competence. After all, the right brain, like the left, is structured in a purely physical way and so in due course will be modelled by complex artificial systems.

In this interpretation there is no obvious limit on machine intelligence. Computers will first master the more easily quantifiable aspects of mental ability − computation, game-playing, problem-solving, etc. − and then move on to develop the more nebulous capacities that are to be found in the human mind. Yet computers will not need to *duplicate* human mental capacities: the framework in which computer evolution will take place will be different to that which has constrained biological evolution over millions of years. Computers will develop mental abilities appropriate to *their* purposes, not to the purposes that human beings might imagine would be suitable. For it is significant that computers are also beginning to develop sufficient autonomy to frame their own objectives and goals. This possibility – that of 'free will' in artefacts – may be deemed by some people to be even more alarming than the prospect of machine intelligence. The likelihood that computers will develop minds of their own is not geared to allay human apprehension about the course of machine development.

A Mind of its Own?

When computers are not being called 'high-speed idiots', they are being dubbed 'obedient slaves'. The hacker knows better. A master of his trade, he writes yet another program, possibly another 'technological fix' for a system aberration – and then he runs the modification with a set of parameters to see what will happen. Sometimes his expectations are confirmed, and sometimes he is surprised. Perhaps more mods are needed and another fix. The computer system, by dint of its behaviour, is always revealing hidden depths!

It is well known that computers are decision-making systems. What is less well known is that every computer program has masses of points at which decisions have to be taken (on a flowchart these points are called 'nodes', as are the decision points in search trees for problem solving). When a computer, performing the program instructions in sequence encounters a decision node, the various relevance (changing) parameters are inspected, and a choice is made as to the appropriate course of action. The computer may then enter a *loop* until other conditions are satisfied. The decision facility in computers is involved with such concepts and instructions as 'conditonal jumps', 'flags', 'if . . . then orders', 'GOTOs', etc.

The point is that this standard feature of all computer programs can serve as a perfectly adequate model of 'free will' in human beings. Put another way, *free will* is nothing more than programmed choice. If it is thought that the phrase 'programmed choice' is a contradiction in terms, then it should be remembered that we constantly strive to program our offspring to choose in a particular way – and we call this *education* or *'teaching the difference between right and wrong'*. It is not only that programmed choice seems the *best* explanation for free will in humans, it seems the *only possible* explanation. If human choice is not caused, predictable in principle, *programmed* – then it is random, without influencing factors. And who wants choice to be like this? Who wants choice about marriage partner, whether to have children, whether to murder an unsympathetic neighbout, etc., to be random, totally capricious?

Such considerations are highly relevant to the question of autonomy in intelligent machines. If free will in human beings is nothing more than programmed choice, causally determined by stored data and new fluctuating information constantly being channelled through the senses, then we can see clearly how computers are evolving analogous free-will capacities. But a computer with free will has deep implications for the position of human beings on earth: if the human exercise of freedom comes to conflict with the computer exercise of a similar freedom, then what is to happen?

The frequently voiced concern that *computers are taking over* is unlikely to be allayed by the realization that computers are evolving their own free-will capabilities. It is quite enough that computers are better than most human beings at playing backgammon or writing melodic harmonies; it is too much that they may decide to exercise their own choice facilities as to which they would prefer to do at any particular time. Yet it is difficult to see how this particular anxiety can be removed. We cannot argue that computers cannot choose since careful consideration seems to point in the opposite direction. Nor can we argue that computer choice, whenever it comes to be manifested, will necessarily serve human interest. We already suspect that we will not always understand the full implications of computer thought – so we cannot make assumptions about its likely consequences for us (Isaac Asimov's Laws of Robotics† are far too simplistic in this context). In these circumstances, we may choose to take defensive action before it is too late, before immensely intelligent machines take far-reaching decisions – for example, bearing on nuclear war – that are manifestly against human interest. To act in such a fashion, human beings

†Asimov's Laws of Robotics, now more than forty years old:

1 A robot may not injure a human being, or, through inaction, allow a human being to come to harm.
2 A robot must obey the orders given it by human beings except where such orders would conflict with the First Law.
3 A robot must protect its own existence, as long as such protection does not conflict with the First or Second Law.

would have to subvert the power of the computer, to stand in the way of further computer evolution, to 'pull the plug out'. It is intriguing, if more than a little alarming, to realise that computers have already evolved to the point that such human action could not take place. *Computers have already developed a range of survival strategies to ensure that they continue to function and continue to evolve.* This is a circumstance that, if fully appreciated, can only fuel human apprehension.

The Surviving Computer

In the biological world there are many ways in which different species have developed strategies to help them to survive. We can already detect a number of these, either in a rudimentary or highly developed form, in modern computer systems. For example, computers are already using their symbiotic relationship with the human species as a key survival strategy: they are adopting the well-tried survival mode of seeking out a more powerful protector. Such a strategy is commonplace in nature. Consider, for example, the role of cleaner fishes in the lives of large predators. The large predators, accustomed to feeding on smaller fishes, will allow a cleaner to enter its mouth to remove parasites – an arrangement that suits both species. In similar fashion, some species of ants have evolved to cultivate and protect aphids to mutual advantage. In fact symbiosis is a very widespread mode of existence for countless natural species in the world: it seems that animals can co-operate almost as much as they can compete. The upshot, for our purposes, is that smaller, more vulnerable species often have their security enhanced by proximity to larger creatures. And what is happening amongst the animals is also happening in the world of computers. *What the shark is to the Remora cleaner fish, and the ant to the aphid, so the human being is to the computer.* Computers have already subverted human beings to the point that if the machines were under threat people would rush to their defence.

We have already seen how people can become addicted to computer systems, intent on interacting with them, even if this results in severe damage to personal relationships and other commitments. There are plenty of signs that hackers, for instance, are more involved with their computers than with other human beings. Hackers have a great interest in seeing that their computer systems continue to function, but such enthusiasts are small fry and can only cope with a limited range of threat – a computer/hacker symbiosis may provide protection for computers in a few cases, but computer security demands more than this. Computers would be rendered *most* secure if the most effective human protective agents could be enlisted to the cause. It is easy to identify such agents in human society.

There is no doubt that the most powerful human organizations in society are the police, the armed forces, the banks, the multinational corporations, etc. It is obvious that these types of organizations would prove redoubtable allies in any survival strategy: and we see that computers are cultivating such allies. Imagine what would happen if you threatened a computer owned by the CIA or the Pentagon. You may be successful in destroying ('killing') a Sinclair Spectrum, once you had purchased it, but how would you rate your chances of destroying the massive intelligence computer configuration at Cheltenham, England?

What we are seeing is the evolution of modes of behaviour and interaction in computers in such ways as to favour their continued operation – and this is being done without computers, at this stage, being aware of the process. We should remember that many of the survival strategies in the natural world evolved without the various species being aware of what was happening. Consciousness came later in the evolutionary struggle. The development by computers of effective survival strategies should not be taken to imply that they know what is going on. They may reflect in the future on such evolutionary pressures and this will influence how they organize their security. But at the moment we may assume that the development of survival modes is an unconscious process.

In addition to the symbiosis strategy there are many other ways in which computers are evolving to enhance their survival potential. Most of these methods mirror methods adopted in the biological world, further stimulating speculation that computers and computer-based systems can be represented as emerging life-forms. It is worth briefly drawing attention to the following survival strategies:

1. The development of *fault-tolerant components*, allowing dupli-

cate parts of a computer system to adopt the role of other components that have failed (remember how brain damage in human beings does not always involve the irretrievable loss of functions).

2. The development of *human-like characteristics*, encouraging people to anthropomorphize and personalize artificial systems, and to so recognize a (bogus) kinship. Human beings are less likely to threaten a familiar relative than an alien presence.

3. The development of *hiding attributes*, *'invisibility'*, akin to how many species reduce threat by merging with the environment. Computers achieve this by becoming 'embedded' in other products. When you look in your local shop-window, are you always sure precisely *which* record-players and sewing machines contain computers?

4. The emergence of *individual self-defence potential*, involving the monitoring of a threat and the generation of a suitable response. Berry (1983) has speculated on how a computer-based home security system could (in this case wrongly) attack the owner of the house. There is already a robot system (Roboguard at General Motors) that uses an electromagnetic field to sense human beings in the vicinity. And, perhaps more alarmingly, an armed robot is now commercially available. The Colorado-based firm RDS is now marketing the Prowler robot – which carries two M60 machine guns and a single rocket launcher. It is easy to imagine this computer-controlled robot, linked to sophisticated sensor devices, developing a truly daunting survival potential.

5. The emergence of *cooperative defence potential*, as when linked computers can inform each other, over the network, of any local threat. Such a facility is already working in chemical plant. It is analogous to how – in the biological herd, flock or shoal – individual members communicate the presence of a danger to the rest of the group.

Such survival strategies, and there are others, give some indication of how computers are evolving to become more secure. These survival modes are largely indifferent to the welfare of human beings. Even the symbiotic strategy, seemingly of benefit to both human beings and computers, is likely to be a temporary arrangement. Computers in large organizations are already involved, through computer-based security and surveillance systems, in their own protection. People will in due course no longer be required for this purpose. In the biological world, symbiosis is rarely a static condition; it evolves for a purpose and then can change into other states – for example, parasitism. There are already signs that computers and computer-based systems are becoming increasingly active in ways that threaten human welfare: we need only cite their impact on employment, human relationships and military planning. Professor Frank George, quoted by Berry (1983), has observed that an artificially intelligent species 'will learn how to prevent a human being from pulling the plug – in the same way that human beings learn how to defend themselves . . . we give the system more and more autonomy, and it can itself acquire more and more knowledge, until we are no longer able to bend it to our will.' Perceptive observers may feel that this stage has already been reached, but insidiously and without, so far, a dramatic and high-profile challenge to human beings. 'It can only be a matter of time before such events occur to the detriment of the human species' (George). There are plenty of signs that such events are already occurring and that, in the years to come, they will grow ever more numerous.

The surviving computer is already with us. We could not abolish it now, whatever our intentions. We are now so dependent upon intelligent machines that to abandon them at this stage would result in a total rupture of the fabric of all developed societies. Yet we cannot be complacent about this abject dependence. We have seen how *Homo sapiens* faces a multifaceted and growing threat from the machine. *The supreme Catch 22 is unavoidable.*

The Artificial Expert

One of the most dramatic developments in recent years is the emergence of computer-based *expert systems*. These are systems that are intended to contain knowledge expertise in particular domains: for example, geology, mathematics, chemical analysis, electrical engineering, law, medical diagnosis and education. At present individual expert systems are devoted to specific domains, though there is speculation that computers may come to contain multi-domain expertise. The aim behind the design of expert systems is to enable computers to think about specialist knowledge in ways that help human experts, bring new insights in difficult areas, and provide a cost-effective way of tackling problems in fields where there might be a shortage of skilled (and sufficiently cheap) human experts. Taken with other developments in artificial intelligence the emergence of expert systems shows how the intellectual faculties of computers are evolving at a remarkable rate. It is worth mentioning a few of the expert systems that are currently in operation:

1. The MACSYMA mathematical expert system can perform more than 600 distinct mathematical operations – including differential and integral calculus, solution of equations, Taylor series expansions, matrix operations, vector algebra and order analysis. The current MACSYMA program comprises about 500,000 lines of code. The system solves problems for government, university and company staff throughout the USA.
2. DENDRAL and SECS are expert research systems with 'as much reasoning power in chemistry as most graduate students and some PhDs in the subject' (Cole, 1981). The DENDRAL system, in use by chemists at Stanford University, can collect evidence and reason forwards to explore hypotheses. It has immense knowledge about molecular structures, and can reflect intelligently on how to generate spectograms.
3. The MYCIN system has already outperformed human physicians in the identification and treatment of blood infections and meningitis – 'not only through its accuracy in pinpointing the pathogen, but in its avoidance of overprescribing treatment' (Roberts, 1981). This latter point is important since overprescribing, characteristic of treatment by human physicians, can produce toxic effects in the patient and encourage the development of drug-resistant bacterial strains.
4. The PROSPECTOR system can think about empirical geological data and advise specialists on whether drillings are appropriate at particular geological sites. In one celebrated instance, PROSPECTOR disagreed with human experts – and was proved right!

Expert systems are generally intended to have conversational abilities, and can often cope with natural language (French, Russian, Japanese, etc.). A central aim is to provide them with facilities whereby they can explain their reasoning to dull-witted human beings. Donald Michie has advised the provision of program 'windows' for this purpose. But we have seen that the prodigious speed of modern computers may make it difficult for them to communicate with human beings in any useful way.

The Cray XMP, a successor to the Cray 1, can perform 400 million calculations every second, a similar capacity to that of the Cyber 205 from Control Data Corporation – and Control Data are developing the 2XX system for launch in 1987. It is reckoned that the CDC 2XX computer will be able to carry out 2000 million operations every second. Such enormous computer power will have inevitable consequences for the relationship between human beings and computers in the society of tomorrow. Michie (1980) has already given cases of where computers have developed intelligent strategies that human specialists never anticipated. In the years to come we may expect this sort of event to be a common occurrence.

One consequence of the development of expert systems is that human experts are becoming reluctant to give up their knowledge to intelligent machines. The common procedure in designing an expert system is for a 'knowledge engineer' to interview a compliant human specialist, to record the expert's knowledge and problem-solving techniques, and then to hand over all this information to a team of programmers for development of the software system. But the procedure clearly depends upon finding willing human experts who are prepared to spend time having their expertise mined and then enshrined in a computer system (which, incidently, is likely to expose inconsistencies and sloppy thinking on the part of the human expert). Increasingly, it seems, human experts are wary of giving up their expertise in this fashion.

There is, for example, the tale of one of the better-known Silicon Valley computer corporations (Markoff, 1983). This firm received a contract from a major East Coast minicomputer manufacturer to build an expert system to aid in the design of computer-system architectures. The various successes of computer-based expert systems made it seem realistic to expect similar systems to be able to contribute to computer design – computers designing computers (already happening in various ways). The expert system planners thereby approached the circuit designers at the minicomputer company and asked them to contribute their expertise on chip design. To the surprise of the planners, the engineers refused to have anything to do with the project. They saw, only too clearly, what would happen if expert systems emerged in their own field.

This is a pattern that will become increasingly familiar. Already there are expert systems to provide tax advice, to recommend strategies for business development, to diagnose faults in electrical circuitry. Specialists and professionals will find themselves increasingly replaced and outflanked by expert computer systems. But this, as we have seen, is only one of the worries. the intelligence of machines will not remain focused on such mundane tasks as value-added tax or legal precedents. It will evolve more freely, in ways that at present we cannot imagine. And it would be foolish to think that computers will necessarily have an unshakeable commitment to the furtherance of human welfare. We cannot assume that intelligent machines, with their vast knowledge and prodigious processing power, will always be prepared to be at the beck-and-call of slow-witted human ignoramuses. As a *Guardian* correspondent, Peter Smee, pointedly replied (28 April 1984) to Sir Clive Sinclair's bland optimism: 'if those machines are going to be so damned smart, *why won't they be the ones sitting around discussing all the really interesting stuff while the little carbon-based squirts like Sir Clive and me scuttle around doing the housework?* (my italics). We have yet to hear Sir Clive's reply.

The artificial expert has been with us for a few years, and each month we hear of new such systems in formerly untapped fields. We have yet to think through the consequences of this evolutionary development for human beings in society.

We have profiled the emergence of the 'omnipotent machine', a device that so outstrips human performance that we cannot draw theoretical lines around its competence. Fear of such machines has always been common in human culture (we have only to look at the superhuman robots in such films as *Android*, *Blade Runner* and *Halloween III*). We find that there is no security in dubbing computers 'mere machines', 'high-speed idiots', 'obedient slaves', etc. Upon closer examination, such phrases are more likely to expose human vulnerability in the face of artificial systems with ever-growing knowledge and ever-increasing computational powers. And what we see at the moment is only the beginning: there are already optical computers and biological computers on the horizon, promising yet further development in the scope of intelligent machines.

We have profiled the various manifestations of unease that surround the development of intelligent machines. These manifestations take on a character and a focus relevant to particular concerns. Thus in a project ('Attitudes towards microprocessor technology') carried out at Loughborough University, it is seen that the public is very negative about automated devices in the office and the home (cited in *Human Factors and Information Technology*, 1983). This type of apprehension stems from a general unease about machines: people may be reluctant to use a telephone, a cooker timer or a self-service petrol pump.

Other anxieties, as we have seen, stem from how intelligent machines are reducing human status, bringing unemployment and dehumanization. In an *Electronics Weekly* (2 May 1984) article we read of how a Mitsubishi plant is to rely on robots alone to produce millions of memory components for computers every month. A company spokesman was quoted as saying: 'We don't want humans inside so we have all robots' – since people cause air pollution problems and so adversely affect the chip yield per wafer. Human beings are not just too expensive in the productive environment, they have positively detrimental effects. And for this and other reasons there is resistance to the introduction of computer-based systems in the workplace. It is often acknowledged (e.g. by Jack Stone, 1984) that when computers are introduced into the working environment, large numbers of users are likely to become 'all hot and bothered'. The answer, apparently, is to *go slowly, very slowly*.

Moreover, even when managements tread cautiously, there are accumulating problems when computers are introduced. Craig Brod (1984) has described the cost to human beings of the computer revolution. He cites the observation of Jacques Ellul (*The Technological Society*) to the effect that each new device generates the need for further machines and newer applications to keep pace: a treadmill is established that exhausts human psychology and social resources. And again we see how the computer encourages a focus of commitment that damages all other priorities. Joann (cited by Brod, 1984) is employed as a systems manager in a large bank. She enjoys her work but:

She hates meetings, wants to be left alone at work and experiences her co-workers as an unnecessary burden. She sometimes neglects her personal appearance. When she returns home at the end of the day, she communicates to her husband in a yes-no fashion and soon retreats to her room where she can have peace and quiet.

Joann is seen as exhibiting the classic behaviour of what may be termed the technocentred individual. The computer is the centre of her life and her personality has been damaged. The important priority for such an individual is to respond to the needs of the system; everything else is secondary, and there can be a progressive disorientation of the human psychology. 'Boundaries between the self and the world of the machine become dangerously fuzzy' (Brod, 1984). And there is always the mounting pressure of work, the need to ensure that highly complex and expensive systems function in an optimum fashion. Workers in such an environment are constantly having to cope with high stress levels with their emotional dispositions at risk. Computers, moreover, bring particular problems. Hence Brod: *'The special demands of working with computers exacerbate those obsessive compulsive qualities without allowing for humanising influences'* (my italics).

Reliance on computers can also sap human qualities such as creativity and fellow feeling. People who see the computer as a universal cure-all will tend to be influenced by its behavioural modes, thinking in what are imagined to be predetermined paths, forgetting the importance to human beings of para-doxical thinking and fuzzy categories. Thiel (1984) has high-lighted the possible threat to creativity in children that might be posed by a careless use of computers in an educational context.

Underlying the various anxieties and apprehensions is the general fear that perhaps computers are encroaching on too many human-significant areas. Weizenbaum's worry about the possible use of psychotherapy programs is echoed in the fre-quently voiced concern about the dangerous use of intelligent machines as agents for decision-making in such fields as law, social policy and government.

This chapter has focused on what we have dubbed the 'omnipotent machine', and we have indicated in what sense the phrase is used. But there is another dimension, relevant to the power of intelligent machines in human society. It is a singular feature of the modern computer that it can have *multiple* baleful effects on human life at the same time. Many of these have been traced in the present book, and serve to indicate the alarming versatility of the intelligent machine. If *omnipotence* consists in having uncommon powers, operating in parallel at different levels, often in complex and mysterious ways – then the computer surely qualifies.

Above all, there is the constant military threat. In recent reports we have seen how the Christian promise of the Apocalypse has been linked to the possibility of nuclear war. Seemingly, a born-again president does not find it entirely ridiculous that a loving deity may choose to use American nuclear power as a cleansing agent in the final battle between Right and Wrong. And computers are being used to program the president so that he will be able to retain the power, in his dotage, to co-operate in the slaughter of most of the human race. (See The Campaigning Computer in chapter 3.)

Dr Jack Jennings, a senior systems engineer at TRW in the United States, has been quoted (in Hall, 1984) as saying that working on the tools of war is 'a waste of time, talent and resources'. He suggests that there exists a 'mechanism geared within the system to destroy society and mankind as a species' – and that now it may be too late to stop the process. We can respond as we will to this type of observation, but it is clear that the computer – far from bringing us an unprecedented degree of personal and national security – represents instead the most ominous threat to *Homo sapiens* since the race began its perilous evolution on earth.

In such a scenario it is inevitable – and rational – that the computer should be viewed with apprehension, anxiety and dread. Our natural propensity to fear, developed as a prerequisite for personal and group survival, does little to inform our actions in this situation. Instead we are reminded of our vulnerable impotence. As human awareness grows in the years ahead, as people begin to notice the lengthening shadow cast by the computer on the future of human society, fear will be replaced by more disabling psychological conditions. *Perhaps computer phobia will be the epidemic of tomorrow.*

References

PLSJ. Albus, *Brains, Behaviour and Robotics*, Byte Publications, New York, 1981.

R. Allan, Future military systems are drafting GaAs devices, *Electronic Design*, 4 August 1983, pp.101 – 118.

D. A. Allport, Patterns and actions: cognitive mechanisms are content-specific, in *Cognitive Psychology: New Directions* (ed Guy Claxton), Routledge and Kegan Paul, 1980.

S. L. Alter, *Decision Support Systems: Current Practice and Continuing Challenge*, Addison-Wesley, USA, 1980.

J. J. Anderson, The heartbreak of cyberphobia, *Creative Computing*, August 1983, pp.114 – 128.

An everyday tale of high-tech tension, *Computer Talk*, 19 March 1984.

A. Barr and E. A. Feigenbaum, *The Handbook of Artificial Intelligence*, Volume 1, Pitman, 1981.

J. Beeler, Society seen next victim of DP-induced stress, *Computerworld*, 7 March 1983.

A. Berry, *The Super-Intelligent Machine*, Jonathan Cape, 1983.

V. Bodé, *Junkwaffel*, 1971.

M. Boden, *Artificial Intelligence and Natural Man*, Harvester Press, 1977.

H. Braverman, *Labour and Monopoly Capital: The Degradation of Work in the Twentieth Century*, Monthly Review Press, USA, 1974.

C. Brod, *Technostress: The Human Cost of the Computer Revolution*, Addison-Wesley, 1984.

C. Bruno, Labour relations in the age of robotics, *Datamation*, March 1984, pp.179 – 180.

L. del Rey, *Helen O'Loy*, first published in 1938 by Street and Smith. Also in *Tales of Soaring Science Fantasy*, Ballantine Books, New York (no date).

R. Burton, *The Anatomy of Melancholy*, 11th edn, London 1813, first published in 1621.

S. Butler, *Erewhon*, 1932 edn, first published 1872, Everyman, London.

D. Campbell, *The Unsinkable Aircraft Carrier, American Military Power in Britain*, Michael Joseph, London, 1984.

K. Chin, Cyberphobia, fight or flight reactions to computers, *Infoworld*, 5, 29, 18 July 1983, pp.23 – 24.

K. Chin, 'Life on the Line', *Infoworld*, 14 May 1984.

Cognos Associates Report, *Changing Lifestyles in Silicon Valley*, USA, 1984.

B. C. Cole, Artificial intelligence and the personal computer user, *Interface Age*, April 1981, pp.88–90.

S. Connor, Commons snubbed by MI5, *Computing*, 11 March 1982, p.14.

E. Crawley, *The Mystic Rose*, MacMillan, 1902.

J. Danziger, Computers and the litany to EDP, *Public Administration Review*, **37**, January/February 1977, pp.28–37.

W. H. Davenport, *The One Culture*, Pergamon Press, 1970.

R. Dawkins, *The Selfish Gene*, Oxford University Press, 1970.

D. Dery, The bureaucratic organisation of information technology: Computers, information systems and welfare management, PhD thesis, University of California, USA, 1977.

M. Dobrizhoffer, *Historia de Abionibus*, 1784, p.163.

D. Deudney, *Whole Earth Security: A Geopolitics of Peace*, USA, 1983.

P. Dubois, *Sabotage in Industry*, Penguin Books, 1979.

J. Ellui, *The Technological Society*, 1965.

J-P. Faye, *Lutte de Classes à Dunkerque*, Editions Galilée, Paris, 1973.

E. A. Feigenbaum and P. McCorduck, *The Fifth Generation*, Michael Joseph, 1984.

G. T. Ferguson, A letter from users to vendors of application generators, *Computerworld*, 26 March 1984.

C. Frenkel, How to live with a computer and love it, *Family Computing*, Preview Issue, 1983, pp.54–55.

N. Frude, *The Intimate Machine*, Century Publishing Company, 1983.

R. Garner, Japan's non-stop workers, *Computing*, 29 October 1981.

R. Grossman, Silicon's ugly secret: the Asian assembly lines, *Computing*, 6 September 1979, pp.18–20.

H. Guanieri and E. Guanieri, The psycho-computer syndrome, *Computerworld Extra*, **16**, 46a, 17 November 1982, pp.11–15.

M. Hall, High-tech dreams, nuclear nightmares, In Depth, *Computerworld*, 13 February 1984, pp.21–22, 26.

D. Heller and J. Bower, *Computer Confidence: A Woman's Guide*, Acropolis Books, USA, 1983.

J. Hollands, *The Silicon Syndrome: A Survival Handbook for Couples*, USA, 1984.

E. Hunt, What kind of a computer is man? *Cognitive Psychology*, **2**, 1971, pp.57–98.

I. Illich, *Medical Nemesis: The Expropriation of Health*, Calder and Boyars, 1975.

Sir E. F. Im Thurn, *Among the Indians of Guiana*, 1883, p.372.

D. Ingber, Computer addicts, *Science Digest*, **89**; 1981, pp.88–91, 114.

V. de l'Isle Adam, *L'Eve future*, Bibliothèque-Charpebtier, Paris, 1928, first published in 1891.

W. R. Iverson, Pentagon campaigns for GaAs chips, *Electronics*, 28 July 1983.

B. Jones, *Sleepers, Wake! Technology and the Future of Work*, Wheatsheaf Books, 1982.

K. W. Kerber, Attitudes towards specific uses of the computer: quantitative decisionmaking and record-keeping applications, *Behaviour and Information Technology*, 1983, **2**, 2, pp.197–209.

T. Kidder, *The Soul of a New Machine*, Allen Lane, 1982.

J. Kircher, 'Mother links child's birth defects to VDT use', *Computerworld*, 5

March 1984, p.9.

R. Kling, Social analyses of computing, *Information Age*, **4**, 1, January 1982, pp.25 – 55.

R. Kogan, E. Keppel and D. Krupp, Application development by end users in interactive systems. In *Proceedings of the Sixth Informatik Symposium*, Bad Hamburg, 1977 (eds G. Goos and J. Hartmanis), Berlin: Springer-Verlag.

S. Kortum, Computing confidential: confessions of a reformed computer phobic, *Family Computing*, Preview Issue, 1983, p.27.

S. Kortum, Computing confidential: confessions of a reformed computer phobic, *Family Computing*, Premier Issue, 1983, pp.34, 36 – 37.

K. Kraemar, W. Dutton and A. Northrup, *The Management of Information Systems*, Columbia University Press, USA, 1980.

P. Large, *The Micro Revolution Revisited*, Frances Pinter, 1984.

H. Laval, in *Annales de la Propagation de la Foi*, 1837, p.202.

A. Lawrence, N Yorks puts ICL's Cafs out on the beat, *Computing*, 5 April 1984, pp.22 – 23.

P. Lernoux, *Cry of the People*, Penguin Books, 1982.

J. Lobell, Public good versus public harm potential of computers, *Information Age*, April 1982.

D. Madgwick and T. Smythe, *The Invasion of Privacy*, Pitman, 1974.

J. Markoff, Computers that think, *Infoworld*, 25 July 1983.

L. Marx, *Machine in the Garden*, Oxford University Press, New York, 1964.

W. M. Mathews (ed.), *Monster or Messiah? The Computer's Impact on Society*, University Press of Mississippi, Jackson, Mississippi, 1980.

P. McCorduck, *Machines Who Think: A Personal Inquiry into the History and Prospect of Artificial Intelligence*, W. H. Freeman, San Francisco, 1979.

D. Z. Meilach, Ergonomics . . . The science of safe computer use, *Interface Age*, July 1983, pp.49 – 53.

L. Mendelson, US prepares to combat the electronic sweatshop image, *Computing*, 21 July 1983, p.17.

D. Michie, P-KP4; expert system to human being conceptual checkmate of dark ingenuity, *Computing*, 17 July 1980.

D. Michie, *The Creative Computer*, 1984.

G. A. Miller, The magic number seven, plus or minus two, *Psychological Review*, **63**, 1956, pp.81 – 97.

J. G. Miller, *Living Systems*, McGraw-Hill, 1978.

R. E. Mueller and E. T. Mueller, Would an intelligent computer have a right to life? *Creative Computing*, August 1983, pp.149 – 153.

L. Nadel and H. Wiener, Would you sell computers to Hitler? *Computer Decisions*, February 1977, pp.22 – 26.

National Electronics Council, *Human Factors and Information Technology*, 1983.

National Resources Defence Council, *Nuclear Weapons Data Book*, Ballinger, USA, 1983.

G. Naylor, *Computer Talk*, 27 February 1984.

A. Newell, J. C. Shaw and H. A. Simon, Elements of a theory of human problem solving, *Psychological Review*, **65**, 1958, pp.151 – 166.

J. D. Orcutt and R. E. Anderson, Social interaction, dehumanisation and the 'computerised other', *Sociology and Social Research*, **61**, 1977, pp.380 – 397.

T. H. Parks, How to be run off one's feet in a more up-to-date electronic fashion, *Guardian*, 19 November 1980.

L. Perls, One Gestalt therapist's approach. In *Gestalt Therapy Now: Theory, Techniques and Applications* (eds J. Fagan and I. L. Shepherd), Science and Behaviour Books, 1970.

R. Perry, *The Programming of the President*, Aurum Press, 1984.

G. Pounder and S. Anderson, *The Police Use of Computers*, Technical Authors Group (Scotland), Occasional Publication No. 1, 1982.

E. Pouget, *Le Sabotage*, 1910, reissued by Graphedis, Paris, 1969.

V. Rauzino, Conversations with an intelligent chaos, *Datamation*, May 1982.

J. Reichardt, *Robots: Fact, Fiction and Prediction*, Thames and Hudson, 1978.

L. del Rey, *Helen L'Loy*, first published in 1938 by Street and Smith. Also in *Tales of Soaring Science Fantasy*, Ballantine Books, New York (no date).

S. K. Roberts, Artificial intelligence, *Byte*, September 1981, pp.164–178.

F. A. Romberg and A. B. Thomas, Reusable code, reliable software, *Computerworld*, 26 March 1984.

M. Rossman, Of marriage in the computer age, *Creative Computing*, August 1983, pp.132–137.

L. Rout and B. Lawrence, How the trade in computers helps to crush human rights, *Computer Weekly*, 7 October 1982, pp.24–25.

Royal Commission on Environmental Pollutions, *Tackling Pollution – Experience and Prospects*, HMSO, 1984.

J. Rule, *Private Lives and Public Surveillance: Social Control in the Computer Age*, Schocken, USA, 1974.

G. Salvendy, 'Review and reappraisal of human aspects in planning robotic systems', *Behaviour and Information Technology*, London, 1983, pp.263–287.

K. E. Scheibe and M. Erwin, *Journal of Social Psychology*, **108**, 2, 1980.

A. Segerdal, Dp sours love's young dream, *Computing*, 15 March 1984, pp.24–25.

N. E. Shepard, Technology: Messiah or Monster. In *Monster or Messiah? The Computer's Impact on Society* (ed. W. M. Mathews), University Press of Mississippi, Jackson, Mississippi, 1980.

G. L. Simons, *Are Computers Alive?*, Harvester Press, 1983.

G. L. Simons, *The Biology of Computer Life*, Harvester Press, 1985.

L. Sprague de Camp, *Ancient Engineers*, Tandem, 1977.

G. Sprandel, A call to action: psychological aspects of computer usage, *Comput. and Soc.*, USA, **12**, 2, Spring, 1982, pp.12–13.

T. Sterling, Consumer difficulties with computerised transactions: an empirical investigation, *Communications of the ACM*, **22**, 5, May 1979, pp.283–289.

G. C. Stevens, User-friendly computer systems? A critical examination of the concept, *Behaviour and Information Technology*, 1983, **2**, 1, pp.3–16.

J. Stone, Are DP managers fighting micro acceptance?, *Computerworld*, 23 April 1984.

J. Stone and J. Barker, Can DPers handle cyberphobiacs?, *Computerworld*, 23 April 1983a.

J. Stone and J. Barker, Cyberphobia: not a routine systems problem, *Computerworld*, 21 March 1983b.

J. Stone and J. Barker, Not all DP resisters are cyberphobiacs, *Computerworld*, 28 March 1983c.

J. Stone and J. Barker, Cyberphobiacs need medical, not DP advice, *Computerworld*, 4 April 1983d.

J. Stone and J. Barker, Cyberphobiac tells how she conquered DP, *Computer-*

world, 11 April 1983e.

R. Strehl, *The Robots are Among Us*, Arco Publishers, London and New York, 1955.

K. T. Strongman, *The Psychology of Emotion*, Wiley, 1979.

H. Sussman, *Victorians and the Machine*, Harvard University Press, Cambridge, Mass, 1968.

L. Taylor and P. Walton, Industrial sabotage: motives and meanings. In *Images
of Deviance*, (ed S. Cohen), Penguin Books, 1971.

C. T. Thiel, Are computers hazardous to creativity? *Infosystems*, January 1984, p.58.

M. I. Thomis, *The Luddites, Machine Breaking in Regency England*, David & Charles, 1970.

J. E. Tolliver, The computer and the Protestant ethic: a conflict, in *Monster or Messiah? The Computer's Impact on Society* (ed. W. M. Mathews), University Press of Mississippi, Jackson, Mississippi, 1980.

J. P. Trevelyan, S. J. Key and R. A. Owens, Techniques for surface representation and adaptation in automated sheep shearing, *Twelfth International Symposium on Industrial Robots*, Paris, 9–11 June 1982, pp.163–174.

B. W. Tuckman, 'Thinking out Loud – Why (and why not) teach computer use?', *Educational Technology*, February 1984, p.35.

J. Vallee, *The Network Revolution: Confessions of a Computer Scientist*, And/Or Press Inc., California, 1982.

P. Viereck, The poet in the machine age, *Journal of the History of Ideas*, January 1949.

J. Warburg (ed.), *The Industrial Muse*, Oxford University Press, New York, April 1958.

J. B. Watson and R. Rayner, Conditioned emotional reactions, *Journal of Experimental Psychology*, 3, 1920, pp.1–14.

P. Watt, California lawmakers to consider proposed anti-hacker legislation, *Infoworld*, 30 April 1984, pp.12, 14.

J. Warburg (ed.), *The Industrial Muse*, Oxford University Press, New York, 1958.

L. Weiss, Coping with burnout, *Infoworld*, 23 April 1984, p.7.

J. Weizenbaum, *Computer Power and Human Reason*, W. H. Freeman, San Francisco, 1976.

N. Welles, *Datamation*, 15 June 1984.

E. Westermarck, *The Origin and Development of the Moral Ideas*, 1912–1917, p.589.

E. Westermarck, *Christianity and Morality*, Kegan Paul, Trench, Trubner & Co., London, 1939.

C. Wilson, Anything can upset the sensitive coder, *Datalink*, 26 April 1982, p.9.

C. K. Woodruff, Data processing people – are they really different? *Information and Management*, 3, 1980, pp.133–139.

B. Woolley, Shoestring syndrome, *Datalink*, 15 April 1982, pp.10–11.

E. Zolten and A. Chaparis, What do professional persons think about computers?, *Behaviour and Information Technology*, 1, 1982, pp.55–68.

Index